FLEX
ABILITY

FLEX
ABILITY

A Story of Strength and Survival

Flex Wheeler

with Cindy Pearlman

Hay House, Inc.
Carlsbad, California • Sydney, Australia
Canada • Hong Kong • United Kingdom

Published and distributed in the United States by: Hay House, Inc., P.O. Box 5100, Carlsbad, CA 92018-5100 • *Phone:* (760) 431-7695 or (800) 654-5126 • *Fax:* (760) 431-6948 or (800) 650-5115 • www.hayhouse.com • *Published and distributed in Australia by:* Hay House Australia Pty Ltd, 18/36 Ralph St., Alexandria NSW 2015 • *Phone:* 612-9669-4299 • *Fax:* 612-9669-4144 • *e-mail:* info@hayhouse.com.au • *Published and Distributed in the United Kingdom by:* Hay House UK, Ltd. • Unit 202, Canalot Studios • 222 Kensal Rd., London W10 5BN • *Phone:* 020-8962-1230 • *Fax:* 020-8962-1239 • *Distributed in Canada by:* Raincoast • 9050 Shaughnessy St., Vancouver, B.C. V6P 6E5 • *Phone:* (604) 323-7100 • *Fax:* (604) 323-2600

Editorial supervision: Jill Kramer • *Design:* Tricia Proctor
Interior photos: Courtesy of Flex Wheeler

Library of Congress Cataloging-in-Publication Data

Wheeler, Flex.
    Flex ability : a story of strength and survival / Flex Wheeler with Cindy Pearlman.
    p. cm.
    ISBN 1-40190-173-5 (Hardcover) — ISBN 1-40190-174-3 (Tradepaper) 1. Wheeler, Flex. 2. Bodybuilders—United States—Biography. 3. Bodybuilding. I. Pearlman, Cindy, 1964- II. Title.
GV545.52.W44 A3 2003
646.7'5'092—dc21

2002154316

Hardcover ISBN 1-4019-0173-5
Tradepaper ISBN 1-4019-0174-3

06 05 04 03   4 3 2 1
1st printing, May 2003

Printed in the United States of America

*This book is dedicated to God;
to my beautiful wife, Madeline;
and to my children—with love*

CONTENTS

Acknowledgments xi
Prologue: The Beginning xiii

PART I: STRUGGLE

Chapter 1: "Man, He's Small!" 3
Chapter 2: Teenage Wasteland 13
Chapter 3: Transitions 25
Chapter 4: Officer Wheeler 31

PART II: STRENGTH AND STEROIDS

Chapter 5: Underwear and the Man 37
Chapter 6: My First Time 41
Chapter 7: Second Best Isn't Good Enough. 49
Chapter 8: Love and Loss 65
Chapter 9: "You May Never Walk Again" 79
Chapter 10: Trying to End It All 93
Chapter 11: "He's Back" 103
Chapter 12: A Life-Sized Action Figure. 107
Chapter 13: Love and War 113
Chapter 14: The Fame Game 119
Chapter 15: Sweating It Out 127
Chapter 16: Discovering a New World 133

PART III: SURVIVAL

Chapter 17: Running on Miracles. 141
Chapter 18: By the Grace of God 149
Chapter 19: Winner Takes All 155
Chapter 20: The Bottom Drops Out 167
Chapter 21: Am I Going to Die? 173
Chapter 22: The 10th Percentile 179
Chapter 23: Olympia 2002 183

Epilogue 191
Flex's Life-Training Tips 195
About the Authors 199

✧ ✧ ✧

Picture a mountain range with sloping ridges, dramatic peaks, and sudden valleys. A thin river of water runs down the middle, separating two massive formations that appear to be made out of solid rock.

This isn't a natural wonder created by a higher power—it's just a man. The "mountain range" is champion bodybuilder Flex Wheeler's back. This sort of perfection is only achieved by a sculptor's chisel . . . or by thousands of hours spent with steel barbells, enduring hours of pain and buckets of sweat.

"Flex Wheeler is a fantastic champion. He has won the Arnold's Classic many times, and I have found him to be an extraordinary athlete. He trains very hard, and he's also a very likable guy. He is a winner," says movie star and pioneering bodybuilder Arnold Schwarzenegger, who goes on to add, "Of course, Flex came through that horrible accident. . . . He overcame injuries and pulled himself together to come out on top. I admire him as a man and a bodybuilder."

Flex Wheeler is tough on the outside, but inside it's another story for one of the greatest bodybuilders of all time. Born a five-pound premature baby, and feeling lost and small inside after a childhood of repeated sexual abuse and hope-crushing poverty, this remarkable athlete found that lifting his <u>life</u> to great heights was the most challenging exercise of all.

This is his story.

✧ ✧ ✧

ACKNOWLEDGMENTS

First, I would like to thank my Lord Jesus.

To Madeline: I wouldn't be here without you. I love you—
you're my whole heart.

To my beautiful children: I love you and am so proud of you *all.*

To my brother Michael; sister, Sharalene; and entire family:
You are my foundation. To my brother Darnell: We've come
a long way together, and I look forward to our future. Thank
you for the offer of life. I love you.

To my grandmother, Ethel Wheeler: You were God-sent.

To Robin Chang: Thank you for being you. I love you.

To my training partners, Big Rico and G-Man: Thanks for
your support.

To my fans: Dare to dream.

To my friends at Hay House: Thank you for allowing me to
tell my story.

To Cindy Pearlman: I love you with all my heart.

To you and yours: God bless!

— Kenny "Flex" Wheeler

PROLOGUE

The first time I tried to kill myself, I was 14 years old. I drove my wobbly red moped—with its rusted chrome rims and flickering headlight—onto the highway, planning to dart in front of the biggest truck I could find and just end it all. I fantasized that I'd become a human shooting star, sliding off into oblivion.

Mother Nature cooperated fully with my plan. My hometown of Fresno, California, was in the middle of the major storm that usually hit us every winter. My grandmother called it the "crazy storm," and she claimed that God sent it to clean up our collective acts. I pretended that that was a loony idea, but inside I felt the thrill of being surrounded by what was unpredictable and dangerous. I also loved a good storm because it was like the whole world was new again and all the ugly stuff simply washed away. Instead of the thick valley smog, I could clearly see the beautiful mountains of Yosemite with their jagged ice caps glistening in the twilight of the bruised sky.

Even better was what I *couldn't* see due to the thick sheets of rain: Gone were the dilapidated houses, gone were the liquor stores on the corners, and gone were the worry lines on the faces of welfare families who tried to feed five kids on $15,000 a year. On evenings like this, people weren't just black, white, or Latino—they were poor saps trying to make it through the night.

Or *not* make it, as was my case.

By the way, maybe I should introduce myself. I'm the jerkoff who was trying to become human roadkill. Back then, I was Kenny Wheeler—4'8" inches tall, 90 pathetic pounds, hair the color of midnight, deep brown eyes. I was a freshman in high school who was flunking every subject. And now I was about to flunk *life*.

I don't mean to be overly dramatic, but frankly, Hollywood couldn't have come up with a better death scene. In fact, I could see the *ABC Afterschool Special* now. . . . *A kid has just heard the most devastating news of his entire life—a local girl smashed his world by telling him that she was having his baby. Driving aimlessly around town in shock in a lightning storm as fierce as what was going on in*

his brain, he saw the highway, which was lit up by the crackling elec-
tricity shooting across the sky. He felt the pull—and found a way out.
He was freezing cold, a real sad sack shaking like a leaf in soaking
wet jeans and a Starsky and Hutch *T-shirt, which was bleeding red*
dye number four down his arm. Somehow he remembered the warn-
ings of his mother, and he ripped out the windbreaker he had wadded
up in his backpack and shimmied into it. . . .

Yeah, I know what you're thinking. The last thing I needed while trying to kill myself was to catch a cold, right? But after a few seconds of hard rain, the cheap nylon jacket was practically glued to me, so it didn't really help. And even though my nerves were jumping, my adrenaline was pumping, and my pulse was pounding, I still shivered and quaked. Dread is always a cold feeling, and it was even more chilling mixed with wind gusts that helped make the road dangerously slick. To top it off, I was thinking about my grandmother, so my hot tears were making it really hard to steer my moped.

I pictured her sitting in the kitchen, smiling and making plans for my future. I imagined walking into that old room with the faded-yellow daisy wallpaper, and I saw my lame self pretending to be totally immersed in getting a glass of milk. In my mind's eye, I could see my grandmother look up, just knowing in her heart and soul that something was very wrong. "Kenny, what is it?" she'd say. "It can't be that bad, baby." But I simply could not fathom my lips forming these words: "Grandmommy, I'm going to be a daddy."

And so, ignoring the DO NOT ENTER signs, I drove the wrong way up the off-ramp of Highway 41. The 18-wheeler trucks flying by me sent ripples of fear down my wet spine, and rocks began to pelt my baby-soft face. It hurt so bad that tears began to stream down my face. Operating on some sort of overdrive, my mind ignored all of this to calculate the next move . . . that's when I realized what a fool I was.

The moped could be kicked up to 25 miles an hour, max. If I didn't get in front of a truck fast enough, the driver would just slam on his brakes, and I'd get messed up really bad. Maybe I'd have to wear a ski mask for the rest of my life because I'd be horribly disfigured. On the plus side, I'd for sure land in the hospital and miss a few days of school, and everybody would be happy that I lived. Of course, I'd probably be grounded for the rest of my life. I'd be 50 years old, sitting in my ski mask in my room, going, "Can I come out now? Can I at least watch TV?"

Swerving into the right-hand lane, I looked for a way off the highway. Now it was official—I was a coward. I just couldn't do it. Like I said, I flunked everything else—now I was flunking death, too. I started to cry harder, and my tears mixed with the rainwater and bright streetlights to the point where my vision became a prism of blurry sparkles. I pretended I was in heaven, but I was really in my own private hell. There was only one thing to do. I begin the slow ride home, which gave me time to think. That's always the most dangerous thing of all.

My troubles began in 1979, after a boring Sunday morning at church. My grandmother, Miss Ethel Pearl Wheeler, wanted to give her favorite young man a special treat. Forget Sunday dinner at home, 'cause we were going to eat out.

By the way, my siblings and I found *home* to be a relative term, since our mother raised us when she could, and our father lived far away (in Oakland, California). That meant that most of the time, my two brothers, sister, and I were under the firm but gentle command of our grandmother, a wonder woman who'd long understood lean times because she'd had 12 sisters, 2 brothers, and later my father to support. Even though times were always tough, Grandmommy was our family's rock, although you wouldn't know it by looking at all 5'4" and 130 pounds of her. Born in 1908, she had powder-white hair that she'd mold straight up to the heavens like she was a female Don King. She usually wore a gargantuan navy blue overcoat, and white Ronald McDonald-style orthopedic shoes that stuck out a mile. And she'd never worn a bra in her entire life, due to the fact that those things were "too damn expensive," and she could hold anything or anyone up with sheer willpower. She was a complete original.

As she got older, her face started to sag a little, so it looked like Grandmommy's lips were fixed in a permanent smile—and that expression reflected her eternal optimism. This woman spent a lifetime making all the major decisions in our family, including buying the Wheeler family's home base on Jensen Avenue. Sometime in the 1930s, Grandmommy took two crisp $20 bills out of her little red pocketbook and shook some white real-estate man's hand, which gave her the ownership of a two-bedroom house the color of pink cotton candy. It was always warm, clean, comfortable, and inviting. If a hungry man passed by the front porch and looked up longingly, Grandmommy wouldn't invite him in (she was a cautious woman), but instead would sweep us kids into the house and bring the man a tray of food and some sun-brewed iced tea. Nobody went hungry on her tiny piece of land, and that was a fact. It was also my safety zone in so many ways.

I loved the feeling of that house, and the hundreds of grinning photos of me taken there prove it. One thing about Grandmommy—the woman loved a Kodak moment. But there isn't one photograph from my boyhood days that doesn't include at least one of her body parts getting in the way—her foot, her elbow, a few strands of that white hair—because she wasn't letting any of her babies stray too far away from her.

I couldn't do anything wrong in Grandmommy's eyes. If I broke a lamp or a glass, she'd just shake her head, chuckle, and say, "Why, we didn't need that silly thing anyway. We're rich in so many other ways, baby."

That last part wasn't entirely true—after all, Grandmommy only made so much cleaning the houses of rich people. After an entire day of digging in their toilets and kneeling in their scuzzy bathtubs, she'd take three buses and then walk three miles home before she called it a day. There was no door-to-door service for her. The idea of getting a car? Well, that was for the families you saw on TV, like the Bradys with their fancy brown station wagon. Grandmommy's transportation was her own two feet, which helped her try to obtain that promise of "The American Dream."

On Sundays, after praising the good Lord and giving a dollar to the church, my grandmother figured that she deserved to get waited on, which is why she frequently took me to eat at Weinstocks department store in Fresno. A shabby but clean restaurant was located inside the big store that was filled with things we couldn't afford. Yet through some miracle, Grandmommy got a store credit card, so when we'd eat, she'd say, "Kenny, the sky's the limit! Order anything you want, baby."

This was our Spago, although the most expensive dish on the menu was meatloaf for $2.99—dessert and unlimited Coke refills included. After we ordered off plastic menus coated in a thin layer of grease, the food would arrive on chipped ceramic dishes—but for us, it was pure joy.

The thrill began when I'd throw open the glass door to the restaurant, and there would be a table waiting especially for us. Grandmommy never disrespected anybody, which is why people treated her like the Queen of Sheba. "Oh, Mrs. Wheeler!" the hostess would exclaim. "How are you on this lovely day? Is your regular table by the window satisfactory?"

We were living like rich folk, and it was heaven. I especially loved how the waitress would come back to our table to check out the situation. "Everything okay, hon?" she'd purr to me.

It was beyond okay—it was the best.

"It's cool," I'd say, wiping the ketchup from my chin with one of the many thin paper napkins I'd use. At that point, the waitress would smile at me warmly, because I was that good boy who escorted his sweet grandmother to Sunday meals.

But one day, Grandmommy and I were at the bus stop waiting to go to Weinstocks when a ten-year-old boy walked over to me with a purposeful stride. Before I knew what he was doing, he slipped a crumpled piece of paper in my hand. It was a little strange, because he didn't say a word—he just turned around and ran onto the bus as if his feet were on fire. Finally, I looked down at the paper, and it had a phone number on it and a name: *Medusa.*

I glanced up at the boy, who was sitting next to his sister, the one presumably named after the Greek devil woman with snakes for hair. She gave me a little wave, so I did the only thing that came naturally: I looked down at my shoes. Out of the corner of my baby browns, I snuck a peek at "the other woman"—my grandmother. She gave me a stern stare back, as if to say, "You know better than that, Kenneth. We don't need this trouble in our lives. Don't we have enough?"

I should have thrown that note away. But since I was just an ignorant kid, I put it in my pocket. That night while my cheeseburger was happily gurgling around in my stomach, I picked up the phone and made the worst call in my short time on Earth. What followed can best be described as basic "birds and bees": Medusa invited me over, and we attempted to "do it" in her tiny pink bedroom. I'm not sure if "it" was right, because we didn't even speak. We just started kissing, and my Sears jeans with the messed-up zipper came off and . . . well, you know. I wasn't yet 14, she was 15, and neither of us really knew what the hell we were doing.

Afterwards, I did the only thing I could think to do under the circumstances, which was to bolt upright, pole-vault into my clothes like a firefighter, and sprint for the door, all the while tripping over her Barbie Dream House. If the track coach ever saw me move that fast, I'd be the star of the freaking team. I was butter sliding across a pan; I was Jesse Owens. I just had to get out of there—and *fast*.

I should tell you something about me, and I should probably tell you right now, 'cause this part is no joke. When I was with Medusa, that wasn't my first time. Let me explain: When I was five, two of my babysitters raped me (although I didn't know what that word was back then). You see, my mother had to go out one evening, so she called my 14- and 16-year-old female relatives to come watch me. After they pissed and moaned about it for about an hour, they finally gave up, because my mom could be very persuasive that way.

After Mom left the premises, the put-upon girls suddenly weren't so bored with the whole baby-sitting deal anymore. "Kenny, let's all play a game," they cooed.

I was thrilled that they weren't ignoring me or making fun of me. However, the next thing I knew, both girls were naked, and they were taking off all my clothes including my underwear. This didn't feel right, but I wasn't so sure if it was wrong. It wasn't until later that I realized exactly what had happened. They didn't just fondle me, they guided me into places I'd never been before. I was afraid. And after that happened, my mind was messed up when it came to this boy-girl stuff. For me, sex was mixed with shame.

Yet Medusa and I managed to do the deed for about six months, as my 14th birthday came and went. Then she started to get on my last nerve. Really, I tried to get rid of her in a nice way, but she wasn't going anywhere. She'd call me up and ask to see me, and I'd tell her that if she really wanted to come over, she'd better sneak in through the window of the garage that my cousin had converted into a bedroom for me and my brother Darnell. I thought if I made it really complicated and she had to ruin her Calvin Klein knockoff jeans to get to me, then maybe she'd figure, *Who needs all this hassle?*

I couldn't believe it, but I'd see her slithering around the yard like some sort of snake, and then she'd be sitting on my little twin bed. I worried that we'd get caught, but once things started happening, somehow all that worrying wasn't enough to stop the main event.

One night, though, something snapped—I'd had enough. So, I just told her, "Put on your clothes and get out! I don't want you bugging me anymore!"

She got the hint, but she was also hurt. That's when the hang-up calls started happening on a regular basis. One night I actually heard her voice on the phone, which delivered some really bad news. "I'm pregnant, Kenny," she announced.

Okay, maybe I was a little dense back then, because all I could think to say was one word: *"How?"*

Sure, I'd taken sex ed in school, but it seemed like it was all about insects and flowers. Our teacher tried to make gardening sexy, which made us kids laugh and pass notes with drawings of bees with boobs. Somehow, the bees in these lectures never had to think about "accidental" bee babies.

Medusa was certain that she wanted to get rid of the baby, so she barked, "I'm having an abortion, and you can't stop me!"

Now I didn't exactly know what an abortion was, but I did sort of gather that she wouldn't be pregnant anymore. And it turned out that I had to help.

"You gotta go on a bus with me real far away and go to this doctor," Medusa said, and then click went the phone.

"Okay," I muttered, too late in more ways than one. I didn't show up on abortion day because I was too scared, and later Medusa called to scream at me. I told her that I just couldn't go killing babies, and that was the last I heard from her for a few months. I could finally breathe . . . or so I thought.

Understand that back then Fresno was a town where the whispers were as loud as screams. For months I heard the rumors: *They said that some 15-year-old girl was still pregnant. It couldn't be Medusa . . . or could it?* I'd wonder. But then I figured that there were plenty of girls who could be knocked up, and not knowing gave me some sort of relief. *At least there's a chance I could cheat this thing. Hey, it could work out, right?* Yeah, right. In church, they spoke of miracles, and no one needed one more than I did. I figured that I didn't have that many sins under my belt. Maybe God would give me a "get-out-of-jail-free card," like the kind you got in Monopoly.

That brings us back to the "last" night of my life. On that night of "the crazy storm," something snapped in me that was as angry as the thunder and lightning outside. I had a sneaking suspicion that I wasn't getting my miracle. But I needed to know the truth, even if I could barely lift my rain-soaked hand to ring her doorbell.

Some answers are a long time coming, and others are as sudden as a smack in the face. The minute the door opened, I knew. Medusa's stomach was huge, hanging over her jeans and stretching out her white Disneyland T-shirt. This was a tiny girl who should have been in her bedroom doing her homework and talking to her girlfriends about her crush on Michael Jackson, but she couldn't dream little-girl dreams anymore. And it was my fault.

On the other hand, I knew how to act like a real baby. "Whose is it?" I demanded.

Medusa stared down at her belly and then glared up at me with pure hatred. "The baby is yours!" she screamed, slamming the door in my face.

At that moment, I could only think of one person—my grandmother. This news would wipe the joy from her smiling face and would suck the very life out of her. This wasn't a worry that would go away—this baby would be a *forever* worry. That's when I looked up, saw the highway, and knew what I had to do. I'd just kill myself. That way, at least, I'd never have to see that look of disappointment in my grandmother's eyes. . . .

When I couldn't get the moped up to speed on the highway, I managed to steer my sorry self to the off-ramp. I got off and sat in the mud as the rain poured down hard. Half an hour passed, and I only sank deeper into the mud. Now the real depression set in, because I was a teenage father and a coward to boot. I couldn't even kill myself, my jeans were filthy, and I missed my curfew, which meant that I was probably going to get some really bad punishment, such as missing *Star Trek* for the rest of the month. My life was in the toilet.

When no other options presented themselves, I finally rode home, parked in the driveway, and gathered the courage to step through Grandmommy's front door. But the minute I did, the worst possible thing happened—I ran smack into my family.

๏—๏

In front of me sat my father; his current girlfriend, Crystal; my brother Darnell, who was a year older than I was; and of course, Grandmommy. The TV was blaring, but as my father looked away from *Bonanza,* his eyes seemed to focus like a laser on my face. His look was a mix of curiosity and disgust.

"Boy, what's wrong with you?" Daddy shouted as Little Joe hugged his dad on TV. Of course, Little Joe wasn't telling his pops, "Oh, when I was out there roping and riding, I got this girl pregnant, and I tried to kill myself tonight by riding my horse in front of a wagon, and I've spent the last hour sitting in the mud wishing that the earth would suck me to its core." All Joe had to deal with was a Mustang with a lame leg, while *I* had a lame life.

"Nuthin's wrong," I finally muttered.

Crystal looked at me and seconded that opinion, because the last thing she wanted was anyone investigating me—that was *her* job. "Leave him alone, Webster. Nothing's wrong," she said in a fake cheerful voice that made my skin crawl.

"Are you crying?" my father persisted.

"No," I said sheepishly, unable to meet his gaze anymore.

My father and I barely spoke to each other, so this particular conversation wasn't unusual. Old Crystal was another story, however—she always made me feel uncomfortable. Maybe it was the way she looked at me . . . and she was always looking at me in that way.

"Nah, he's not crying. It's just, you know, raining outside," Crystal said, shaking a Kool out of her pack and lighting up. She had a way of blowing smoke in the air that made it look like the house was on fire.

I couldn't take it anymore, so I ran past the cloud of fumes into my bedroom. I sat and cried for a long time, realizing that getting run over was a really dumb idea. *What was I thinking? It would be much easier to just shoot myself.* And suddenly I remembered that my 16-year-old sister had a gun in her room. I cleaned up my face, walked into her room, and casually asked, "Sharalene, do you still have that gun? Could I just see it for a minute?"

Sharalene, who was hiding the gun for one of her boyfriends, was so irritated by the interruption from her *Seventeen* magazine that she probably wanted to pull out the weapon and use it on me herself. With disgust, she looked up from the fall hairstyles page and yelled, "Boy, *get out of here!*"

I ran out of her room and locked myself in the bathroom, where I cried harder—until I noticed something interesting in the form of an economy-sized bottle of aspirin. By now I was getting better at this killing-myself stuff, so I calmly poured some water into the cheap Scooby-Doo mug somebody'd gotten for free at the gas station. I snuck the aspirin and water back to my room in the garage, and in the dark, I immediately swallowed as many chalky pills as my hand could hold. Then I reasoned that one fistful might not be enough—I might still be alive in the morning. So I swallowed another hand-ful. Wanting to barf, I willed myself to remain still by thinking about the most boring things possible (such as the specifics of my math homework) until my stomach settled down.

I waited to feel a sharp pain, keel over, and die, but that didn't happen. *What a rip-off!* I thought. At this point, there was really nothing else to do but sit on my bed and wait for death. As usual, I closed my eyes before I turned on my tiny nightstand light. I always kept my lids shut tight when I first flipped on the lights in order to give the cockroaches a few minutes to go back into hiding. Bugs were one thing I would *not* miss in the afterlife.

I sat down on my bed and waited for something to happen. Again, I felt nothing—and that's when I got very scared. I wished that I hadn't taken the aspirin, but now I was just going to have to go with it. I'm not exactly sure if I passed out or just fell asleep, but later on,

I saw my grandmother standing over me with the bottle of aspirin in her hand. She was a silent blur, because even though my brain seemed to be working, I could barely see or hear. The entire world was fuzzy, as if someone had stuffed a cotton towel in my head.

From the way my grandmother was acting, I knew something crazy was going on. She was shaking me and yelling for someone to call my mother, who lived just a few blocks away. The next thing I remember is being dragged into the bathroom. I wanted to scream at my relatives to stop, because I was dead. I had disappeared—I was the *late* Kenny Wheeler.

Next thing I knew, I was in the shower, and freezing-cold water began to pound my ultrasensitive skin as my mother and grandmother stripped my clothes off. I heard them insist that my father's girlfriend, Crystal, get out of the bathroom, but she didn't want to leave (which was a shock to everyone but me).

"Leave! Now!" screamed my mother, but this witch just wouldn't budge.

I started coming back around, and the first thing I saw was Crystal staring at me in that sick way of hers. I knew that the last face I saw couldn't be this woman's, so I blocked her out mentally. From that point on, I just focused on my grandmother and my mother, who were hysterically screaming something about "hanging on."

"Kenny, fight to stay alive, baby!" Grandmommy screamed.

I didn't want to fight—as a matter of fact, I was all for giving up. Unfortunately, my plans were ruined when the ambulance arrived and the pros took over. Two paramedics dragged me out of the shower, placed me on a stretcher, and tried to put an IV in my arm. All the way to the hospital they were trying to poke me with it.

"Stop! Damn, that hurts!" I cried.

"That's a good thing, son," one of them said. "You can feel again."

You're breaking every vein in my damn arm and that's a <u>*good*</u> *thing?* I thought. It figured that I got two goofs who obviously flunked paramedic school. But they must have been doing something right because, slowly, my brain power returned, and soon I heard an earful, as the doctor and my mother started arguing next to my hospital bed.

"What caused this to happen?" the doctor demanded.

My mother, who was virtually being interrogated, said, "He has this new girlfriend—maybe he got in a fight with her."

Now this was the final insult. I got really upset. After Medusa, I had the good sense to start dating Levetta, a beautiful, doe-eyed girl who was almost five feet tall and as sweet as they come. She was a year older than I was, and my brother Darnell had seen me staring at her one day on the bus. He practically lifted me to my feet by my belt loops, saying, "Don't punk out." Because this sounded like a dare, I boldly went up to Levetta and asked for her phone number. She didn't slug me; in fact, she wrote her number on my arm in blue marker and 'fessed up later that she thought I had a nice booty. We were cooking with Crisco!

No one could say a bad word about her—not even over my (almost) dead body. So, instead of voicing my anger in the hospital, my blood pressure said it all for me by rocketing off the charts, which caused the doctor to throw everyone out of the room. Finally, I had a moment to close my eyes and take a deep breath.

I know what you're thinking. Why haven't I mentioned Levetta before, right? Well, we have a lot of chapters left to go. You're also probably thinking, *I guess the little jerkoff lived.* Well, it's obviously not a corpse who's telling you this stuff. I can tell you that my body not only survived, it also saved my life. Eventually, the package that God gave me created a new existence—this 90-pound weakling would later flex quite a bit of muscle.

Now when I'm on the workout bench, grunting and moaning as I lift 500 pounds of pure steel, my mind is free to wander. The cold metal reminds me of being that boy with the weight of the world on his shoulders. . . . But before we go any further, I need to tell you about him.

PART I

STRUGGLE

Chapter 1

"Man, He's Small!"

Just about anyone who's been blessed with a child will tell you that the birth of their baby was one of the biggest deals in the world. The key word for my arrival, however, is *small*. If there had been a contest for the scrawniest baby delivered at Fresno Community Hospital on August 23, 1965, well, let's just say that the blue ribbon would have been mine . . . and it would have covered most of my five pounds and seven ounces.

The nurses doted on me, yet as far as I know, none of those lovely ladies remarked, "He's going to be a great bodybuilder someday." I'm pretty sure that if any of them *had* said those words, they would have been carted off to the psycho ward.

It's funny how often what we are at birth is nothing close to what we turn out to be. For example, my legs looked utterly useless because they were as thin and translucent as chicken bones—but someday those same legs would only wobble when they asked a girl out or when they hoisted 500 pounds. Yet when I was born, those leg muscles could barely lift their own weight, and my arms were two fleshy toothpicks held together by a roadmap of veins. If there were muscles in there, well, they sure weren't flexing.

I also think it's interesting that a small baby girl is dubbed "dainty" or "delicate," while the birth of a small boy tends to make the men in the room particularly nervous, as if they got the wrong order at a burger joint. I can just imagine my father saying, "Wait— I didn't order this skinny thing! Bring me the ten-pounder with lots of hair, please."

But Webster Wheeler didn't say those words. Instead, he looked at my mother and then summed up the entire state of affairs with this pronouncement: "Man, he's small!" He said this while shaking the big 'fro that was his trademark. My dad was so handsome that the neighbor women fawned over him, calling him "so fine."

My mother, Gloria, was a striking, five-foot-tall woman with a different wig for every day of the week. "He's a baby. What do you want?" she shot back.

The doctor promptly corrected them both. "He's premature," he said, pleased that he'd been able to keep me alive when it seemed that my tiny lungs might not have been up for the job.

Keep in mind that this was the '60s, before medical science invented all sorts of tubes, wires, and contraptions to help a small baby breathe. Many preemies like myself just slipped away, leaving the family doctor to look helplessly at the parents and say, "We're so sorry. There was nothing we could do."

But this doctor was able to pull me to the land of the living. He smacked my barely-there buttocks and then looked in my big round eyes, which told him that my spirit wasn't willing to give up. After a few anxious minutes that left my mother plenty nervous, the doctor handed her a tiny bundle, saying, "I think we're out of the woods. You should thank God. He really was on your side today." The miracle he put in her arms was a completely bald bag of bones with no meat on him. Hey, it was a start.

No one would have more building to do on a body than I would.

According to Wheeler family lore, my mother took one look at me and said a tiny prayer. Then she added, "He's adorable. Look at that little smile." She was selling it hard, but my father wasn't buying.

A few hours later, Dad decided to give me a chance, because a higher power—his mother—spoke to him. My grandmother came to the hospital, scooped me up, and boldly announced, "He has a bright spark to him. I see great things for this little man." Even after I became internationally famous, there was no question of who my biggest fan was—it was that remarkable woman who became the one stable influence in my young life.

Even though I'd already triumphed by staying alive, life wasn't going to be smooth sailing for me. I was a "surprise" baby, thanks to the fact that my mother's birth control (she swears) failed. She met my father when she was 16 years old and he was a sophomore at Fresno State University on a football scholarship. She proceeded to get pregnant with my brother Michael, so a quick trip to the justice of the peace was in order. Not long after, my sister, Sharalene, arrived; three years passed and my brother Darnell came along; and about 15 months later, I joined the group. By that time, however, my parents were wisely divorced. I don't have any memory of them ever being together as a couple, but the word on the street was that it was "pure TNT all the way, baby."

Naturally, it wasn't easy for Mama to be a single African-American mother in a small town. Back then, Fresno was smack-dab in farm country, and it reeked of cows and pigs—and our house contained the stale, hopeless stink of poverty as well. Understand that my mom did the best she could, but there was just so much she could do. She was only in her 20s, yet she had five kids grabbing at her night and day (oh yeah, my brother Robert came along five years after me). We got by, if you want to call it that, on welfare and by the grace of God—but Mama's eyes were simply numb most of the time (and Dad had already moved to Oakland).

As for me, I didn't get the fact that our situation was so dire. Generally, I was a pretty happy kid, even if I was wrapped up in my own emotional world most of the time. "Kenny is just a sensitive boy," my grandmother would say. "Nothing wrong with it."

It was nothing to brag about either. I remember one night I was watching *Star Trek* with my brothers, and hot-to-trot Captain Kirk was making out with some chick, who incidentally was half green and half purple. At the end of the episode, she had to return to her alien planet to find a half-green, half-purple dude. As the credits rolled, I wept. "But I want them to be together!" I insisted. "Kirk really likes that green-purple girl! Now he has hurt feelings!"

My brothers shook their heads, and Darnell said, "Kenny, next week he'll be making out with a maroon girl, so quit your bawling, you little fool."

I cried harder because my brother called me a name . . . and so it went. My feelings were like raw, gaping wounds that constantly bled.

My sister, Sharalene, said that I was the "sweetest, shyest boy on the planet." She'd say, "Kenny, you're the type of boy who would take the last piece of food on Earth and give it to someone else."

Soon I'd really have something that was worth my tears, because trouble bubbled up each time Mama left the house. By the time I was four, she was hardly ever home at all, which seemed strange since she didn't really have a job. I had no idea where she went during the day or night, but she'd just disappear, leaving instructions that Michael and Sharalene were in charge.

Michael was the disciplinarian, and unfortunately, his power went directly to his head. He wouldn't just beat Darnell and me for our "crimes"—he'd torture us by making us stand near the old-fashioned radiator in the living room. It was this big contraption with thick metal parts that stuck out from the wall like the arms of a monster, and Mama used to always warn me to stay away from it. But Michael would make me stand there until my clothes started smoking. Or I'd sit down for lunch, and Michael would swoop by and take my plate. There was no bargaining: If *he* was hungry, *I* went hungry—and he had quite an appetite.

And then there was my brother Darnell. Once when I was five, we were fighting over something stupid, which is just standard kid stuff, and Darnell, who was always a pretty big kid, got so angry that he picked up a metal chair with a jagged edge and used it to cut my wrist. We were too young and dumb to know that he'd nicked a major vein, but a river of blood pooled on the floor. Darnell told me to "clean up the mess, go outside, and play."

Later on, I wrapped my wrist with a towel and went to the local recreation center, where kids could play with stuff like used bats and balls for free. For me, it was like wandering into heaven.

The director, a very nice lady in her early 40s, took one look at my arm and almost passed out. "My God, Kenny, it's like someone tried to kill you! I think you may have cut a major artery."

She asked me what happened, and somehow I just instinctively knew that I couldn't tell her the truth. "Kill me? Nah! I fell off my bike," I said. I didn't have a bike, but I wasn't giving my brother up—no way.

She ended up rushing me to the hospital, where I got five stitches on my wrist, and then the nice hospital lady asked me for a number to reach my mom. I told her the truth, which was that I hadn't seen my mother in two days. But back then no one called child welfare or made any big moves—they just sent me home and told me to "be more careful." (By the way, I still have the scar from the day I "fell off my bike.")

Darnell's attitude didn't exactly improve as time passed, and the scars he inflicted were visible both inside and out. One day he took me around the side of Grandmommy's house and told me to stand still while he picked up a brick and hit me in the head with all his might. I was knocked unconscious, but no one knew it—they thought I was just taking a nap in the grass. Later on, I stumbled around the house like I was drunk, for I couldn't see straight and kept falling down. Darnell thought it was hilarious then, and years later, he still did. He'd say, "Remember that time when I knocked your head off with a brick?" and convulse with laughter.

Let's just say that we were a dysfunctional family before psychologists even invented that term. And I've saved the worst for last—Darnell's nighttime habits. I guess he didn't like to get out of bed during the night, so he'd just stand up and pee on me while I was asleep. Yet I was always the one who got in trouble. "Kenny, you are not a baby!" Mama would scold. "You cannot pee in your bed." I was just a small boy and didn't even know what was going on—part of me thought that maybe I *was* wetting the bed. But how could this be possible since I still had to pee so badly in the morning? How much pee could one little guy hold?

"Piss pot," Darnell would call me. I figured that maybe I was one, which is why I never accepted sleepovers at any friends' houses. Many years later, Darnell finally told me that he was the pee machine. He did it because he was too lazy to go to the john. I could only shrug, because he was still bigger than I was, and what was a kid who was falling out of the slimmest pants sold to mankind to do?

Speaking of my preteen physique, my sister would look at my backside and tease me in a good-natured way. "We should call you booty-*less*," she'd say after a family trip to K-Mart to buy new jeans for school. And when we were getting along, Darnell and I would stand on the street corner and do poses for the passing cars. I'd make two fists and curl my arms underneath me like I was some muscle man. But the truth was that I was a booty-less boy who was all ribs, knees, feet, and feelings.

But the only time my size truly bothered me was when it came to Mama and her male friends. As a single and quite beautiful young woman, she frequently had dates who visited our home. It's really difficult for a young boy to watch that kind of thing even in the best possible circumstances, which of course, these weren't. Some guys would want to be all nice to us kids like they were our daddies, and that was bad enough . . . but then there were the other types of men. I remember a few episodes where Mama would bring home her date late in the evening, and he'd beat her up.

The worst was a burly cop named Dave who barely spoke. One night he savagely attacked Mama and then went to the fridge, took one of our last bottles of Coke, and went to leave like it was no big deal. Who knows why, but Mama didn't want him to break up with her. "You can't go!" she screamed, grabbing at his legs and desperately trying to stop him from walking out the door. Well, he started hitting her face with the Coke bottle over and over again, causing her to shriek from the pain of her wounds *and* her loneliness—I'm not sure which was worse.

As we heard our mother's cries, Darnell (who was nine at the time) and I (seven) snuck through the house as silent as mice. It was strange because we might have been foes by day, but when someone messed with Mama, we solidly came together as one. That night, we had the same idea, which was to find Dave's gun (which he'd left in our house) and kill the bastard. A stealthy prowl through the dark hallways led us to the Promised Land. Darnell eased open the nightstand drawer, and there it was—the gun was now glinting in the moonlight coming through the curtainless window. I looked at my

8

brother, and he looked at me, then we both stared at the gun, but we were too scared to pick it up. At that moment, I felt as lightheaded as I did that day he'd hit me in the head with the brick. Luckily we didn't have to make a move, because Mama stumbled back into the room, crying and bleeding, but alone.

She still dated the "hands-on cop" after that night, and he even lived with us for a short period of time. Sadly, Mama's big weakness was that she was too quick to forgive. If a man wronged her, *she* was at fault, so she'd give him another chance . . . and another and another. I never understood it, and I still don't—there's no excuse for a man to ever put his hands on a woman in that way. In fact, when I was little, I'd sit on my bed and wonder if there were women out there who got hit and then told the bastard to get out. I also wondered how much longer it would take me to get bigger so I could get these suckers out of our lives with my bare fists.

As a little man, however, I lost most of my battles—including the ones with Fresno's public school system. Sure, I didn't like school, but no one could understand why I got D's and F's while my brothers and sister got A's and B's. Back then I was just called stupid or worse, but it really wasn't my fault—many years later I found out that I had (and still have) dyslexia. I was actually quite clever, 'cause I figured out that if I got in some kind of trouble in class, I'd get sent to the principal's office, which was a perfect way to get out of the embarrassment of doing schoolwork. I'd end up sitting in the office for hours while they tried to call my mother (good luck finding her), or I got a paddling (no big deal compared to what I got at home). A far worse horror was being called on in class. I never had the answer, so I'd say something really rude and then get sent back to the office—it was a vicious cycle.

Later I was told that my trauma at home combined with my dyslexia made it almost impossible for me to excel at anything more than just basic human survival. But back then, my teacher would tell my mother that I didn't apply myself, and she'd shrug as if this was the least of her concerns. So, I was just another kid who had failed in the system . . . or had the system failed *me?*

One part of school was a bright spot for me, however. As small and frail as I was in elementary school, I could do 100 sit-ups a minute. It was almost as if I had a little motor inside me that folded me up and down at double-time speed. Soon the gym teacher took notice and announced, "Look at our Kenny go!"

The other kids were impressed, and my brother Michael even took it upon himself to teach me to do push-ups. I could do so many of them that he'd get tired of counting and would leave the room as I still pushed on up. I became obsessed with working my body, and gradually I started to see tiny muscles forming. Sure, everyone called me "Bony" or "Skinny Kenny," but the simple act of pushing myself physically made me feel stronger on the inside, which is where it counted the most.

One day I wandered into a local karate studio. I knew that I didn't have the money to pay for even one lesson, but oh, how I wanted to be like Bruce Lee! In the movies, he was always the skinny guy who got the bad guys with his lightning-fast feet and deadly, whiplike hands. That day in the studio, I was in awe as I watched the students, and I wondered if there was any way in the world I could just watch a few classes.

I'm sure that Robert Stevenson, the studio's owner, felt sorry for me when I reached into my worn-out jeans and pulled out two quarters as a sort of pathetic bribe. "This is all I have for lessons, but I'll pay you more when I get it," I offered. My eyes were cast to the ground, because there was just no way he was going to turn me into Bruce Lee for 50 cents and a promise.

"Son, welcome to class," he said, taking only one of the quarters.

"I'll pay you back," I promised him.

"I know you will," he said with a smile. "Now, is there some reason you're just standing here and not in class? Get moving!"

It was meant to be, because that night I wandered over to the rec center, and they were playing the movie *Enter the Dragon* for the best price possible—free. I was even more blown away by Bruce Lee, and I desperately wanted to be like him. I was delighted when the rec center started offering free karate lessons. I longed to sign up, but I was only nine, and the poster clearly said that you had to be ten.

"You're obviously a very mature nine, Kenny, which always counts," said the center's leader, giving me a wink and pointing me in the direction of class. Karate was probably the first thing I loved to do, and I was good at it, too. Who would have figured that the skinnier you are, the more flexible you are when it comes to martial arts? Little "Bony" was the only one who could do the splits and high kicks, and it didn't take long until I was the best student in the class.

When I won my first blue ribbon, the other kids actually clapped because they admired me and the one skill I had in this world. Finally, I'd done something right. All I could do was cry.

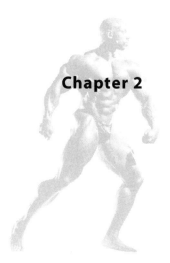

Chapter 2

Teenage Wasteland

When I was 11, life took an interesting turn. My mother shipped me off to live with my father in Oakland so I could "finally get to know him better." The other kids stayed with Grandmommy, so at least I had some peace and safety at Daddy's house. Plus, he had a new wife named Linda, a sweet woman who liked kids and was especially nice to me. Daddy even had a job as the assistant football coach at the local junior high school, which meant that there was some money coming in, but he couldn't be around 24/7 to keep an eye on me.

The dilemma of "what to do with Kenny" after school was solved when my father introduced me to the weight room at his school. "You're too little to go on the field with the football guys. So just stay here and do . . . something," Daddy said.

He picked up a ten-pound dumbbell in one hand and handed the thing to me, and immediately I just about dropped it on his toes. "Kenny, the idea is that you *lift* these things. You don't toss them on the ground or you'll break a bone," said my somewhat annoyed father.

Frankly, it wasn't a bad way to pass the time, and I found myself getting stronger as the months wore on. Soon, that wimpy

10-pounder was nothing, and I was lifting 25 pounds, 30, 50—and so on. It was cool, because my T-shirts started fitting really tight in the arms. And I absolutely freaked one day when I did my muscle-man pose in the mirror and my little baby muscles flexed back.

Life improved in other ways, too. Sharalene and Darnell would visit me at Daddy's, and we formed an unspoken truce not to fight. One Saturday morning, Daddy ripped the covers off all of us and told us that we had ten minutes to be dressed, washed, and in the car, or else. An hour later, we pulled into the parking lot of this amusement park called Great America, and my father plunked down close to $100 on tickets and really tasty junk food. I shoved hot dog after hot dog down my throat, and washed them down with clouds of cotton candy. Walking was out of the question—my heart was soaring to the point that I just had to skip.

At one point, Darnell actually threw his arm around me—which was the closest we'd come to a hug in our entire lives. We eventually ditched Sharalene, Linda, and Daddy and made a deal to only ride the biggest roller coasters, because scaring ourselves silly was the manly thing to do.

"You puke on me and you're toast, Kenny," Darnell said, grabbing me by my collar and drawing me closer while he took his other hand and pretended to give me "noogies" like Bill Murray did to Gilda Radner on *Saturday Night Live*. At that moment, we weren't just brothers—we were friends by choice. True to our pact, we rode every single exciting ride twice. And I never did become toast that day—I kept my lunch down. Darnell appreciated it, and even went so far as to share his waffle-cone sundae with me. Of course, on my last lick, he shoved it in my face, covering my chin in marshmallow fluff.

"My brother's Santa Claus!" he screamed, as my father came closer, accompanied by a slightly peeved Sharalene. It remains one of the happiest days of my entire life.

When I was 13, Mama wanted me back with her in Fresno, so from then on, I only visited my father during vacations. And speaking of parental units, no one wanted to believe it when my nice stepmother, Linda, broke up with my father (for reasons unexplained), and he started dating around.

I stayed with Daddy and his girlfriend, Crystal, a chunky 32-year-old supermarket cashier, the summer before I turned 15. I've already mentioned how Crystal made me uncomfortable. Well, during this particular summer, things got much worse. She'd wait until my father went out with his friends for the night, and then she'd wander into my room, smoking a Kool and telling me stuff I didn't want to hear, like, "You're gonna be a real lady-killer someday." Eventually her hands started wandering around under my covers, and I froze because I wasn't sure what to do. Daddy had made it clear that he really dug her and if I gave her any trouble while he was out, I was going to wish I'd "never been born." Plus, Crystal told me that what she was doing was for my "ed-u-ca-shun."

During that Christmas vacation, I was back with Daddy, who was working an extra job to make some holiday cash. One night Crystal took off all her clothes and climbed under the covers with me—I knew what was happening, but I wasn't sure how to stop it. Afterwards, she warned me that if I told my father, she'd say that I forced her to do it, and I'd do life in prison for rape. I cried myself to sleep that night, as nightmares of going to jail drummed through my mind.

Several weeks later, Daddy and Crystal came to visit Grandmommy, and I noticed that Crystal was spending a lot of time in the bathroom throwing up. I got a little worried.

"I'm pregnant, and I think it's your baby," she told me.

I felt so dizzy that I had to sit down. My entire body trembled with fear for days because I knew that my father was going to kill me . . . or maybe now I really would go to prison.

A week or so later, something strange happened. Crystal came around after a fight with my father, and she took me aside. "You don't need to worry your handsome self. I lost the baby," she said.

I felt guilty and sad because I was happy that this little baby was gone. Deep down I figured that no little person deserves to be born in that much shame. And then, gathering up all the courage I had, I knew what I had to do. The next time she came into my room, I grabbed her hard by the wrist and said, "Get away from me or you'll be with your baby." She never touched me again.

I was starting to discover my power, which I used on those who had hurt me. The following summer, I was enjoying the peace of

Daddy's house when Darnell decided to visit me. Since I was a 15-year-old kid, I naturally spent the bulk of my time on the phone, either with my official girlfriend, Levetta, or another girl I liked named Maria.

Darnell walked in and found me professing my love to Maria. He snatched the phone from my hands and told her, "I used to piss on him and beat him up when he was younger, and he's still a little punk."

Furiously reaching for the phone, I screamed, "Why are you telling her that?"

"Oh, you don't want me to talk to her?" Darnell taunted, hanging up on Maria.

Well, something that had been building up like a volcano in me for 15 years suddenly began to erupt. It didn't help that Darnell next decided to smack me in the face—hard—not once, but twice. I was dazed for a moment, but then everything crystallized, and my eyes narrowed.

I swung at him as hard as I could, and missed. He laughed, which made me more determined, so I threw him to the ground with one hand like he was one of those blow-up punching bags. Even Darnell was shocked that he went down so easily.

I fell on him and began hitting him in the face. Each punch was for a childhood wound, and I found myself healing deep scars as my knuckles connected with his face, shoulders, and mouth. A thin trickle of blood ran down his chin. *Ah-ha!* All those years of karate and lifting weights had paid off—I was nobody's "little fool" anymore. And when he tried to get back up again, I grabbed him and smashed him down. He was so dazed that he looked like a deer caught in the headlights.

Finally, Daddy walked in and broke it up. "I bet you feel good," he said to me. But the truth was I *didn't* feel good. In fact, I was scared by the pure rage that I found inside of me, and I wondered if I could stop myself the next time. One thought kept going through my head: *What if Daddy hadn't come home?*

Even though my mom had pulled me back home, I was pretty much living full time with my grandmother by the time I was 15. It was 1980, and Fresno was changing—it was getting rougher, and gangs were forming in the streets. I tried to avoid trouble by spending every spare moment in a local karate studio called Way of Japan. The training I'd started when I was nine really helped—I had the moves, and my head felt stronger and more together when I was training. The sad fact was (big shocker) that I still couldn't afford to pay for lessons.

One night, owner Bob Halberton took me into his office. He asked me to show him a few moves, but he never asked me to move toward my wallet. When I got done slicing and dicing the air, Bob handed me a uniform and said, "Be here every single day at four o'clock. Don't disappoint me—and most of all, don't disappoint *you.*

To stay out of trouble at night (which was the worst time in our town), my friend Mike and I would hang out in the safety of his gang-free basement. His dad had a weight-lifting set down there, so we began training ourselves.

"Hey, we're bodybuilders!" Mike announced one evening, flexing his muscles in the cracked mirror that his mother was too lazy to throw out.

"We're what?" I asked, sweating in my good school clothes.

"You know, bodybuilders! Jeez, Kenny, read a magazine." Mike cupped his hand over his mouth and whispered, "Mike and Kenny are the winners of Mr. Olympia! And the crowd goes wild!"

I grabbed an empty Pepsi bottle to use for a microphone. "I'd like to thank my fans!" I yelled out, before launching into makeshift poses. Eventually we collapsed on the ripped, dusty couch, laughing hysterically.

Unfortunately, I couldn't avoid the bad influences of the streets forever. Call it peer pressure . . . or stupidity. It wasn't long before I got duped into stealing some money from the register at the local AM/PM Mini-Mart where I'd recently gotten a job. (Sure, it wasn't that great of a job, but that's no excuse.)

The incident began with a guy we'll call Stupid Davy, who thought that we should give ourselves a raise by dipping our hands into the till. One night he grabbed a wad of cash and put it in my backpack. My stomach did flip-flops because I knew it was the dumbest idea I'd ever heard in my life—but it got worse when Stupid Davy said, "I'll be right back to help you sneak it out."

Davy *did* come back—with the police. He lied to the cops, insisting that I'd threatened him and that he'd just run away to get help during the robbery. It turns out Stupid Davy was actually *Greedy* Davy, and he wanted my hours at the Mini-Mart. Who knew he'd be so shrewd as to use this as a way of getting my time?

"Turn around!" the cops barked, clamping my scrawny wrists in cold steel handcuffs.

The next stop was an equally chilly cell in juvenile hall. I sat on a thin, sweat-stained mattress, terrified for my life (even though I was alone in my cell). For some reason, the cops took me out of the general population of prisoners like I was some kind of threat. Later, it dawned on me that the real threat was actually the other prisoners.

Normal bodily functions started to concern me. I didn't want to pee because the cells didn't have individual bathrooms, so the cops would haul prisoners to a group bathroom. Supposedly, they stood outside b.s.-ing each other while the prisoners went in to do their business, but I didn't want to know about the kind of business that went on in there. I vowed that I wouldn't ask to leave my cell, *ever,* even if my insides burst. My stomach started aching from my fear and the now-frantic cry of nature, but I finally fell into a fitful sleep. I woke up the next day ready to die because I had to pee so badly. I willed myself not to think about it.

"Can we bring you some milk?" asked a nice policewoman.

Milk? Oh my God! I thought I might spontaneously start spraying water like a human volcano. "Um, no thanks," I said, squeezing my legs together—I wasn't about to become somebody's bathroom girlfriend.

Later that morning, the steel bars finally slid open, and a very large cop announced, "Kid, you can go. Behave yourself."

All the charges had been dropped, because the cops had finally figured out that the whole robbery was Stupid Davy's idea. Grandmommy, Daddy, and Darnell picked me up, and the three of them found me sitting in the police station among scowling cops and sad-eyed kiddie cons.

In front of everyone, my grandmother hugged me tight. Turning to the men in my family, she said, "Say nothing about this, and don't ask Kenny anything about it either." Leaning closer to me, she whispered, "I love you and believe you."

By the time I got in the car, I was crying, and my grandmother thought of the obvious reasons why. "You must be hungry and scared," she said, smiling warmly.

"No, I really have to go to the bathroom!" I cried.

"Get this boy a burger and a bathroom," she barked at my father, who pulled into the first McDonald's he saw.

I peed for about a week, and then downed two Big Macs, fries, and a small Coke—no need to fill up on liquids.

I thought I was in the clear until I got back to school, but somehow the word had gotten out about my arrest. I was called into my next holding cell—the principal's office. "This is what you get for playing fast and loose with the law," said Mr. Blowhard, showing me my transfer papers.

Unbelievable! I thought. *I just can't win.*

I wasn't a bad kid at all—in fact, most nights I just sat alone in my room, which was no easy deal because, like I mentioned before, Darnell's and my bedroom was once a garage. On nights when the temperature hit 20 degrees, it was so cold that you could ice skate on your sheets . . . although this didn't seem to bother our roomies, the cockroaches who also called the place home. When I was sleeping, I'd feel their tiny feet run over my blanket, so I just pulled the threadbare cloth up over my eyes and clenched them shut as tight as I could.

The peer pressure continued when I turned 16, thanks to the guys I hung out with who liked to steal in the same way that other guys like girls and sports. We'd go to a 7-11, and they'd say, "Hey, Kenny! You better go along with us," even though I wasn't a good shoplifter. In fact, I was one of the worst ever since my fingers weren't sticky, they were shaky. But they were artists when it came to stealing, easily lifting beer, condoms, magazines, you name it.

"Whadja get, Kenny?" they'd ask after we were safely packed in some jalopy that reeked of leaking gas and oil. I'd pull out a single piece of Bazooka gum that I'd lifted from the one-cent basket, knowing how long it had taken me to get up the nerve to pull this heist.

In fact, by the time I got the guts to even do this much, the other guys were usually standing outside the store, looking through the glass window and mouthing the words, "Come on!"

One night the boys were outside a 7-11, and I was inside trying to find something to lift. I went for a Tootsie Roll, which didn't exactly mean grand theft because the thing cost under a buck. Still, it was the best I could do, so I slipped it in the torn back pocket of my jeans.

The next thing I knew, the burly bouncer-type clerk was hovering over me and waving a finger in my face. "I know you took something. Give it to me!" he bellowed.

He let me cop a plea, which meant that if I paid him the 65 cents, I could go free. I reached into my pockets, furiously rifling around, but the only thing that came out was some dryer lint. I was too embarrassed to tell the clerk that I was this poor.

"You little punk!" the clerk barked. "In two seconds, I'm calling the police!"

"Wait," I begged, "I have my lunch money!" I knew I was just buying time because I never had lunch money or even *lunch* on most days. I didn't have a red cent on me, so I broke into a dead run for the door. The bouncer reached out and easily grabbed me. I kicked him hard in the head with a karate move, took off running again, and kept moving right out of the store, past my friends, all the way home. The minute I walked in the house, I went right to the kitchen to throw the candy away. I didn't want it—I'd never wanted it.

I hated my life.

My friends came around later on, promising, "The next time you want something, we'll steal it for you." But I never asked for a single thing, including beer, which they started to drink on a nightly basis. I didn't drink for many reasons, but more than anything, I really did want to be a good kid. It was tough going, to say the least.

One horrible stunt I pulled happened late one night when my posse found some powerful slingshots (wrist rockets) and a bag of steel marbles. We got in one guy's old beat-up car and took off for what we later called our "rampage."

As we whipped those marbles into people's car windows, we were both horrified and thrilled. The shattered glass on the asphalt looked like hundreds of shining diamonds. Then one of the guys shocked us all by pulling out a tiny handgun from his jeans and shooting out a window of a McDonald's.

Soon we became bored, so a couple of the more fearless guys started shooting at *people* with the slingshots and marbles, and we laughed at their shrill screams of pain. "This is crazy!" cried one victim. Peeling out of there, we found a kid on a ten-speed bike and *piiiiing!*—we shot him with some marbles. He actually fell off the bike and into a glass window. We were out of our minds that night, and I'm lucky I didn't get a lifetime jail sentence because of it. Finally, the evening came to a sad end when one of my so-called buddies jumped out of the car and began throwing beer bottles at a house.

"Enough!" I screamed. "You're overboard! And I'm not going to jail because of you!" Finally, I had to threaten to beat the driver up if he didn't take me home immediately, which he agreed to do. The next day, I snuck out of bed, not minding when my bare feet ran across the frosty morning dew on our lawn. It was one of the few times I wanted to be the first to read the morning paper—and there it was in black and white. The headline screamed: 100 CARS SHOT OUT. VANDALISM HITS TOWN. *The Fresno Bee* asked anyone who knew anything about the crimes to call the police, but luckily, no one in town made that call.

(**Note:** For you kids reading this book, I can't say enough times that this wasn't cool. It wasn't even *close* to being cool. Don't go out and wreck stuff for the sake of making your stupid friends happy. You could get arrested. Or worse, you could wind up shot or dead. I don't condone this kind of activity, and it remains one of the biggest regrets of my life. In fact, if one of my children ever did something like this, I'd ground them forever. I'm serious.)

My life of crime climaxed soon after the slingshot incident. I was working at another AM/PM Mini-Mart with my friend Malcolm. He used to give me free washes and gas at the place he worked, but when he got fired from his job, I got him a gig working next to me. Malcolm was into fixing up cars, and I had this old lavender Volkswagen bug (no jokes, please) that needed a ton of work, including a cooler paint job. Both of us were desperate for a quick infusion of cash, and that's when I learned about Malcolm's hobby—stealing money from the store's ATM. He was quite the teacher, because soon he showed me the ropes . . . little did we know that there was a video camera in the corner of the store capturing all of our clever moves.

It didn't take long for the owner of the Mini-Mart to call the police on us. With a loud bang, the cops burst through the glass doors while Malcolm and I were working. One of them said, "Okay, we got you kids! Hands where I can see them."

I truly thought that it was the end for me, once and for all, yet the cop pointed at me and said, "You're not the one we want. We know who showed you how to do this, and that's why he was fired from his other job. We want *him*," pointing at Malcolm. The officer asked me, "Is he the one who showed you how to bust into a cash machine?"

It was high noon: Should I rat out a friend or go to jail? Sometimes there are no easy answers. "Yeah, he showed me," I said.

"Good answer, kid," the cop said. "Your deal is that you pay back the money, or you're going to be sitting next to him in jail."

It was like revisiting that 7-11 where I stole the Tootsie Roll, because, once again, I didn't have a cent on me. This time, however, I was told that I could take a few days to come up with the $5,000 that the machine was owed. *Five grand? I should just check myself into jail and plan not to pee for the rest of my sorry life,* I thought.

When I walked into the house that night, my grandmother didn't even look up from her crossword puzzle. "Kenny, why have you been crying?" she asked. I swear, that woman had a sixth sense about her grandchildren.

I didn't answer her, but later I told my girlfriend, Levetta, "I'm going to jail."

"Why?" she gasped. "Why did you do this stupid thing? Now I won't see you anymore. We have a homecoming dance coming up! Why?!"

I couldn't take it anymore, so I hung up and took the long walk to face Grandmommy, the only real judge in my life.

But once again, she didn't judge. She simply said, "Baby, why didn't you tell me when you walked in?" Then she picked up the phone and called every single person she'd ever had any contact with in this life. Her speech was the same for each one: "I've never asked you for this before, but I need money, and it's an emergency." She never mentioned what I did, or that I was even involved in this mess.

Did I mention that it was actually *beyond* a mess? The cops eventually made me take a lie-detector test to find out the precise amount of money I'd stuffed into my pockets. The nice cop asked me why I needed the cash, and I mentioned car repairs.

"Where did you fix the car, Kenny?" the kind officer of the law inquired.

My motor mouth couldn't stop running, so I said, "Oh, down at Ralph's Auto. They do the best job. Everybody should take their car there." Silly me, but Ralph's had records, and the cops soon had the paperwork for everything I'd purchased: rims, tires, a racing engine. It was 300 bucks here, a grand there.

My grandmother collected every penny I owed from her friends and paid the Mini-Mart owner in cash, while her manner to me was as warm as ever. "I think we learned something here, Kenny. Nothing in this life is ever free," she said.

It was a lesson I'd have to learn the hard way—again and again.

Chapter 3

Transitions

I'm proud to say that I finally learned the lesson that crime doesn't pay; now it was time to be accountable in other areas of my life. Remember Medusa? Well, she *did* have our baby—a girl named Brandy—but I wasn't exactly a model father. In my own defense, however, I was never even told that my baby had been born—I had to hear about it around town. Yet that's no excuse for why I didn't see my daughter for the first two years of her life. If I'd really wanted to, I could have tracked Medusa down and tried to work something out with her . . . but I was too busy just living.

On my 17th birthday, Grandmommy threw me a big party, which was interrupted by a loud knock on the door. Medusa was standing there, holding a wailing little girl and court documents ordering me to pay child support. You see, she'd told the court that I was 21 and was ditching my responsibilities. *Happy birthday to me.*

Once again, Grandmommy took charge. "He's only 17," she told Medusa, "but we want to work this out."

My ex looked dubious when my grandmother invited her and Brandy inside the house. As soon as they walked in, I knew that I had to come to terms with my past. I glanced down at the sweet face of my first child, and I knew she was mine—she looked exactly the way I had when I was little.

"Kenny, this is your baby," Grandmommy said with the kind of importance that world leaders use when they make speeches about the future of our planet. And then she quietly added, "A real man stands up and is accountable when it matters the most."

It was hard for my mind to wrap around the fact that I was Brandy's daddy—but that pug nose, those pouty eyes, and those chubby cheeks told me that she was the next generation. With shaking hands, I held her, while my mind pretended that she was my baby sister and not my daughter. I guess I wasn't ready to stand up that tall just yet.

Months went by and Medusa refused to bring Brandy around again. Strangely enough, this bothered me, but I didn't say a word. Then on my sister Sharalene's birthday, Medusa brought the baby over to celebrate with us. After a few uncomfortable moments, my sugar-sweet ex and I had a vicious argument about how and why she got pregnant: She said I was stupid, and I said she was a slut. So much for the reunion.

"You will *never* see this baby again!" she ranted, storming out the door with my daughter.

I didn't see Brandy again until a few years later. I was at a car wash, and I looked up to see eyes like mine staring back at me. There before me was a little girl in a faded pink dress, holding a little Raggedy Ann doll. To her mom, I said, "Hello, Medusa. Can I have your new number so I can at least call Brandy?"

"Brandy doesn't want to speak to you," said my ex.

I knew that this wasn't the time to lose my cool, so I simply said, "Why don't we let Brandy be the judge of that?"

With some hesitation, Medusa passed me her phone number, and before she took Brandy away, I got down on my knees and touched the little doll my daughter was holding. "She's so pretty—just like you," I told Brandy, who was looking down at her toes just like I used to when I felt small.

As I walked away, I saw that she was smiling, and it broke my heart. Even in my immaturity, I knew that this little girl was already growing up lacking—she didn't have much, and my stepping out of the picture left her with even less. I wondered what she'd say a few years from now when the other kids asked about her daddy. Would she grow up to hate me? I felt bad for myself, but I felt even worse for Brandy, because no little kid should have to be a part of the messes that the so-called grown-ups in her life created.

I was tempted to run back, scoop up my daughter, and apologize from the bottom of my heart, but my feet stayed planted because I was still very young and afraid. So I just watched her fade into the distance. At that moment, I knew that sometimes there aren't enough ways in the world to say "I'm sorry."

In 1983, the universe decided to throw a little "too-bad-about-the-rough-patches" apology in my direction. Through some miracle, I graduated from high school—which only happened because my sister and my grandmother spent time helping me learn to read. They didn't know how to help me conquer my dyslexia, but they did the best they could, and it was, amazingly, good enough. Not only did I get a diploma, but I also muddled through the application to Moorpark College, about 50 miles away from Los Angeles. Grandmommy had saved up some money so that I could go to the school for an official interview. Yet as I sat in the dean's office, I thought it odd that no one seemed too interested in my academic achievements (as if there were any). In fact, the football coach stopped by, sized me up, and said, "Son, good forearms. This could be your new home."

I understood why they wanted me to play ball, because I wasn't just a skinny little kid anymore. Once I got my act together when I was 16, I started to work out every day, alternating between the martial arts training and lifting weights. I was mass and muscle, chest and arms—although I still wasn't a huge guy. Even though I was never that into helmets and touchdowns, I'd played a little bit of football with Darnell on our high school team (go, Edison Tigers!). Anyway, I didn't care—I would have been on the ditch-digging team if it could have gotten me into college.

So Kenny Wheeler from Fresno, the guy with the long, luxurious Jeri curls, went to college with a half-baked plan to be the next star of the NFL. However, my football career was quickly sidelined—on the first day of practice I walked off the field because I simply knew it was time to go home. Somehow standing in that ocean of grass and getting the hell beat out of me didn't seem like so much fun. I'd had enough of those sorts of afternoons when I was a kid, and I just had to get out of there. My mind was screaming, *No more!*

After a lackluster semester where I was beyond broke in Los Angeles, I decided to come home to Fresno, when I enrolled in Four Seasons Commercial College. Levetta, my high school girlfriend, called, one thing led to another, and we began to seriously date each other. And then, a few months into our big reunion, she started to bug me about getting married.

"Baby, I think we should wait. We're only 19 years old," I told her, sounding strangely mature for the first time in the history of my life. It's just that the words "'Til death do us part" kept going through my mind—that seemed like an awful lot of years to stay together.

Levetta wasn't buying into my "let's keep it loose" plan. "Don't you love me?" she demanded through her tears.

I was sunk. I *did* love her, but deep down I had a nervous feeling in the pit of my stomach. Eventually she wore me down, but I insisted that we couldn't get married until we'd saved some cash. Community college didn't really fly with these new plans, so I dropped out of school at age 20 to work in an A&P supermarket during the day and a gas station at night. Afterwards, we got hitched and I moved in with Levetta, who had her own apartment. Things were looking up, although all that legally binding togetherness jangled my nerves at times.

My salvation and escape came from a small, smelly gym called Fitness Plus, where my friend Jeff Lawson began training me in bodybuilding. By the mid '80s, bodybuilding had gotten serious, and I thought it was fascinating. The fitness magazines filled the racks at the A&P, and I'd read them during my breaks. The guys on the cover were huge, and I figured that their paychecks were just as big. They were mountains of men, and I envied them. I wished that someone would put a voodoo spell put on me so that I'd be able to carry their kind of weight—literally and figuratively.

The more I read about the sport, the more intrigued I became. It was different from karate or working out at the gym—it was precisely sculpting the body into a great work of art . . . except one used weights instead of a knife and chisel.

Knowing that I didn't have anything to lose, I began to follow a bodybuilder's workout routine at Fitness Plus. A few months later, my muscles had definition, and I'd packed on a little girth. Even my brother Darnell was impressed with the results, so he decided that maybe he should do something to challenge himself. He become a boxer, which, for him, was just as physical and empowering as what I was doing.

Darnell came to the gym with me one night to check things out and to show me his new boxing moves. "Hey, little bro, let's put on the gloves," he said.

We hadn't fought in years, and I was a little nervous. I knew from experience that he had great hand speed, but now he was taking real boxing lessons, too. *What the hell,* I figured, and stepped into the makeshift ring.

I don't exactly know what happened next. Darnell's fists seemed to be flying at me in slow motion; I could see everything he was about to do with his fists, and I'd slap them down and then strike him. I plowed him with thick and deadly punches to his jaw, and he was shocked. What made it worse is that every single time he looked at me in this stunned way, I'd giggle. I laughed myself silly.

At one point, Darnell's nose started to bleed. "Okay, that's enough, Ken," he said.

"We can go more," I retorted, this time trying to stop the smile that was spreading across my face.

Even my brother got it. "I guess this officially means I can't pick on you anymore," he said, holding out a sweaty, slightly bleeding hand. We shook on it with deadly serious faces, like the leaders of two countries finally declaring peace.

Chapter 4

Officer Wheeler

Officer Kenny Wheeler, reporting for duty.

Yes, believe it or not, the former juvenile delinquent decided to become a cop. In 1986, in a moment of pure inspiration, I decided to enroll in the Fresno Police Academy. It wasn't such a tough gig, but it was an emotional time for me nevertheless. I was 21 years old, and as good as I was at the physical stuff, I still stunk at bookwork thanks to my dyslexia. Other officer candidates just sailed through the written exams, but they couldn't do one chin-up; I could pull myself up all day long but could barely answer an essay question. As usual, I found myself floundering, but at that time, the Fresno Police Academy let candidates pass if they excelled at the physical requirements. I guess they really needed cops that year, and no wonder— the streets were getting rougher and deadlier by the minute.

There was another roadblock when it came to my being a cop. I found it extremely difficult to shoot a gun, but not because I had any moral issues with it. It was just that I was getting more muscular thanks to the bodybuilding, and all the guns were too small for my hands. No one seemed to realize this; instead, the other cops just wanted to pass me off as a "bad shot."

Finally, I was given one of the largest guns at the Academy, a Glock 18. In our final shooting test, we had to hit these metal statues—if we got them in the right spots, they fell backwards and we passed. With my tough-guy gun, I nailed them all, earning the second fastest shooting time in my class.

As for my law-enforcement career, there was just one glitch. I had a terrible driving record because I used to drag race my souped-up lavender Volkswagen with the chrome and fuel injectors—yes, the very same car that nearly landed me in jail because of how I "paid" for the repairs. Anyway, at the time, my goal was to beat the guys in the hot Corvettes and rebuilt Camaros because I was the better driver, even if I did have a less-than-cool ride.

Thanks to all that racing, I had multiple speeding tickets, giving me six points on my driving record (seven meant you lost your license for good), and no one trusted me with a police car. So imagine my surprise when the Fresno Police Department encouraged me to complete my training, promising to hire me as soon I was done.

What I didn't realize was that this would be a "non-street job"— that is, I got to work in the town jail. To put it mildly, this was a very depressing job. At night I'd book drunks and put their sorry carcasses in holding pens while they narrowly missed puking on me. Hating the stale smell of beer, I'd actually hold my breath when I handled them. And the drunks usually thought they were tough guys—when I'd book them, they'd want to touch me, so I'd grab them and simply slam them to the ground. The lucky ones passed out before we could dance.

I was so muscular by then that the creepos started calling me Officer Steroids. The other officers thought that was pretty funny, too, so it became my nickname. For instance, if some guy who liked to beat on his wife got out of hand in jail, I'd hear someone yell, "Go get Officer Steroids." Within seconds, I'd be punching the criminal senseless, while the other cops just laughed and turned away.

Once again, I learned that jail isn't a place for decent people. Race, age, and sex don't matter—it's just the dregs of humanity across the board. Interestingly enough, I found that the women prisoners were always the loudest and the most trouble. I remember once we had this white woman named Roxanne who was really loud and vulgar—she even cackled like a rooster while cussing out everyone. A young black girl, in for a drunk-and-disorderly charge, was thrown into Roxy's cell, and Roxy turned around and called her "nigger." The two women were about to punch each other's lights out, which is when I got the order to set them straight.

"Kenny, try hog tying," said my captain, smiling. Basically that meant that I had to take one lady, pin her to the ground, and hold her on her stomach. At that point, I'd have to grab her hands behind her back and handcuff them to her feet, turning her into a little inside-out circle. Imagine lying on a cold cement floor for hours in that position . . . even that nasty Roxy started to bawl because she was in agony.

I was actually thankful when the economy went south and I got my pink slip. Old Officer Steroids was thrilled to get cut from the force, although the police department promised that they'd hire me again once they found some dough—I hoped it took them forever to find it. By then, all I cared about was training at the gym.

I figured I'd had enough depression in my life. I needed to parole myself from it.

PART II

STRENGTH AND STEROIDS

Chapter 5

Underwear and the Man

At this point, I'd like to switch gears and tell you how I began my love affair with bodybuilding.

It started when I was barely a man. It was 1978—I was 13, and all my buddies were suddenly on me with one of those suggestions that's really an order: "Kenny, you should sign up for this body-building contest at Fresno High, man. They got prizes and everything."

The signing-up part was no problem because (thankfully) there wasn't a fee. Training wasn't a big deal because I was already doing that in my spare time. The worst part of the deal was . . . aw, I just can't say it. All right, the most awful part of the event was figuring out what I'd put on my hide besides a nervous grin.

When it was time to first show the world my bodybuilding skills, I wasn't even concerned about doing the poses or getting stage fright—nah, what was nagging me most is that I couldn't afford to buy anything fancy to wear for the big show. The bottom (pun intended) line was that I couldn't pony up $20 for those fancy silky drawers that I saw on professional bodybuilders.

I'm embarrassed to admit that I did my first show in my under-wear. Now we're not talking about those tighty-whiteys you buy for two bucks a pack—mine were bright blue, but they were still under-wear. Consequently, I felt really exposed, like someone had caught me with my pants down . . . which, in a way, they had. Of course, it didn't really help that it was cold that day inside the Fresno High auditorium, although it very well could have been my nervousness that was making my body tremble. Standing backstage (and I use this word loosely because it was more like a janitor's closet) with kids my age who were much larger, I couldn't help but think, *What the hell are you doing, Kenny? This is not a good thing.*

Since I wasn't one of the first guys invited to the stage to pose, I had to wait a very long time. And then, after what seemed like an eternity, I finally heard, "Next—Kenny Wheeler from the Fresno Rec Center!" The emcee spoke into a microphone that vibrated with each syllable, so it sounded like I was Mick Jagger about to come out and meet his thousands of adoring fans.

I, obviously, was no Mick Jagger. I think I heard about ten people clap, including Grandmommy (of course), yet I had no choice at that moment but to walk out on the stage. The big spotlight they used for school plays was blinding, which was a good thing. I could barely make out the shapes of the people in the audience.

I did hear my brother Darnell scream, "Kill 'em, Kenny, you punk!" which gave me a little energy boost before I did some poses. However, I wasn't a trained bodybuilder at the time; I was just a kid who worked out in his rec center and wanted to be Bruce Lee. So all I could think to do was mimic what everybody else was doing, and my keen sense of observation paid off, because I ended up bringing home a sixth-place ribbon. (Did I mention that there were only seven competitors?) But the prize didn't matter—when I walked off that stage, I felt as if I were high off the ground.

From then on, I couldn't be stopped. I signed up for show after show. The ribbons got better, but somehow that wasn't the point. The real prize was the surge of joy that the shows provided. When you find something that you're good at, and people confirm that you're A-OK, man, it's like getting the ultimate stamp of approval for taking up space on this planet. I continued to crave this recognition as I got older.

Fast-forward to 1986. Around the time that I got laid off from the jail, Fitness Plus offered to officially sponsor me in a show. I really needed the moolah—I could barely even afford the entry fee for the show. But I also needed something else: a name.

Somehow the name *Kenny* doesn't exactly fit well into the bodybuilding world—it sounds like someone's pesky little brother who you want to shove out of the room. *Kenneth* isn't half bad, but it almost sounds a little too scholarly, like "He's a nuclear physicist by day and a bodybuilder by night!" I was puzzled by what I should do about this dilemma until I took Levetta to a family reunion in Bakersfield.

I liked Levetta's family a lot. My affection for them was partly due to the fact that they were a close bunch, but also because the food at these parties was always hot and delicious, and there was tons of it. Levetta's relatives were also really funny, and they were the kind of people who loved to use nicknames—which they tended to do the second they'd sized somebody up.

By now, I was also pretty muscular from all the working out and the shows. "Look at him," said one of Levetta's cousins. "He's always walking around flexing."

At the exact moment that sentence was airborne, one of the uncles rounded the corner to get some food. He took one long look at me and said, "Oh, here comes Flex."

That night everyone started calling me *Flex,* and it just stuck.

A few days later, my friend Steve was helping me get ready for a show. He had the entry form in his hand and asked me, "What do you want me to call you on this thing?"

"Flex," I replied, and it felt good—it felt right.

Steve stopped for a minute to consider it. "Let's see . . . I can see the announcer saying, 'Flex Wheeler is onstage, and the crowd is going nuts!'"

Now it was time for me to add my own two cents: "Here's Flex and his skinny butt walking out there, and no one claps," I replied, always the pessimist.

It's as if I already knew that this new passion of mine would never be an easy one to muscle in on.

♈ ♈ ♈

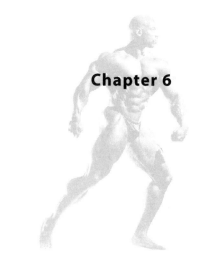

Chapter 6

My First Time

Like many things, it had an innocent beginning. My 18 years on steroids started with a handful of tiny blue pills, which I never imagined had the power to turn me into a rather young corpse.

At first I thought of those pills as a work tool, the same way an accountant needs a calculator or a construction worker uses a hammer. Steroids are simply part of the game in the bodybuilding world, as common as barbells or a high-protein diet.

Of course you never forget your first time. . . . My life changed on an average day while I was working at Copeland's Sporting Goods, where I put in eight hours daily after Levetta and I got married. When it came to my day job, I was basically your average, bored 19-year-old guy still trying to find my way in the world.

One day during the crushing boredom of our shift, a co-worker initiated a little conversation about my hobby of bodybuilding. "So you're *that* guy—the one who's won a few shows," she remarked.

I nodded, smiling shyly back at her, but inside, I felt something a little foreign for a kid with my background. I think it's called *pride*.

"Yep, I'm the guy," I said, puffing out my chest.

Strangely, she didn't want to feel my biceps or have me flex for her. Instead, her interest was of the helpful variety. "You really should talk to my cousin," she told me. "He's a bodybuilder, and he knows *the secret.*"

The secret was *Dianabol,* and it ended up coming from this guy whose name I can't even remember but who was instrumental in my descent into what we call "using" in the business. He didn't even keep the stuff in a bottle—when I met him, he just reached into his faded 501's and pulled out a handful of these pretty little pills. He said, "Hey man, these will help you grow like everything is out of control."

What did I know about health when I was 19 years old? The entire time I was growing up, we couldn't even afford a family doctor. If we got sick, somebody would haul ass to Walgreens to get an economy bottle of aspirin; if we were *really* sick, Grandmommy made us some soup, gave us some Robitussin, and sent us to bed.

I didn't think it was a big deal to take a few tiny pills. I mean, they couldn't kill me, right? I started taking them every single day, figuring that since I was only 140 measly pounds, anything would help. No one was writing about steroids back in the early '80s, but I heard that they were a bodybuilder's friend—and I soon learned why.

I began to notice that something major was happening within my body, and not all of it was good. First of all, my skin started expanding all over, as if someone had stuck a hose in my mouth and pumped me full of air. In fact, my skin became so stretched in certain areas that it had faint lines where it looked like the tissue had torn open—the skin's natural reaction to packing on 20 pounds within a matter of three weeks.

Soon my entire body began to look like a pregnant woman's stomach after a tough nine months. I developed huge stretch marks—which I lovingly called my "worms"—all over my chest and thighs. Speaking of my inner thighs, they grew so big that they almost touched. And when I woke up in the morning, I noticed my biceps bulging before I even flexed. There were worm marks there, too, but who cared? I was suddenly moving into the big leagues, and I was stoked.

I was also constantly hungry—no matter how much I ate, it was never enough. My body was expanding so much that I was becoming a human garbage disposal of junk food. Across the street from

Copeland's was a McDonald's that I'm certain I kept in business, because for lunch I'd order three Big Macs, two orders of fries, two shakes, and a Coke. Two hours later, I'd be starving again. I'd have Levetta stop by with an afternoon snack, but we're not talking an apple or a bag of chips. I could eat an entire pizza at three o'clock and then be ravenous again two hours later.

My face got so fat, puffy, and pimply that people I knew started stopping me on the street to say, "Man, what's wrong with you? You look like someone injected you with a big grease gun."

Hey, it was worth a few zits—I was a bodybuilder, so I had to build my body.

At the time, I was on the outs with my parents, who weren't too thrilled that I'd married Levetta at such a young age. And during those times when my new wife and I weren't on good terms, I'd stay with my grandmother, who had no idea what was going on with the drugs. (She just thought I was getting a little heavy from all the working out.)

But the woman who slept with me noticed that my entire body was growing like crazy, so one night, Levetta summoned the courage to ask the hundred-thousand-dollar question: "I hear these rumors that you're taking steroids. Are you?"

I didn't skip a beat. "No, Levetta, I'm not. What's for dinner? I'm starving."

That same night, I went to the gym, and one of the bodybuilders wanted to talk to me in the locker room. "Flex, try this new stuff," he said, handing me a new steroid called *Deca-Durabolin*. There was only one hitch: This wasn't a handy little pill—it came in a vial, with a big, scary needle in a separate package.

Did I mention that as a little kid I'd throw a tantrum when Grandmommy wanted to take me to the doctor to get my booster shots? I wasn't any more courageous when it came to needles now, but this time I figured I had a good reason for freaking out.

You see, the needles back then that went with steroids weren't little, like the ones that diabetics use to give themselves insulin shots. Needles actually come in sizes: the higher the number, the thinner and smaller they are (which means they're less scary). To put this in perspective, diabetics use a 27-gauge needle; my first steroid needle was a 15. For those not versed in the medical arts, it basically looked like a harpoon. But it was the only way to get this drug, so I went into the bathroom stall of the locker room and slowly loaded the amber fluid into the clear plastic chamber of the needle. Then I sat down and cried for about an hour, just staring at this horrible, painful-looking device.

Finally, I dried my eyes. I took some toilet paper, put some rubbing alcohol on it, wiped a spot on my butt, and attempted to inject the needle in there. My first try was unsuccessful—the needle went in my cheek about one centimeter, no more than if a splinter had entered it, but I was convinced that I'd rammed it clear through to the other side. I immediately pulled the needle out. Realizing that my entire career as a bodybuilder was on the line, I rubbed more alcohol on my rear, and this time rammed the needle in there. I was hot and sweating and my hands were shaking, so I pulled the needle out again. In the process, I shot the fluid all over the floor and wall, which meant that the next few minutes were spent cursing. Loudly.

I could only think, *Oh, my God, get it together. You're really punking out here, man.* A few nervous minutes later, I drew the fluid for the third time. I closed my eyes, stuck the needle in again, and shot it into myself while I broke out in a cold sweat that made me shake.

That's how I began taking the shots, which I took weekly for almost two decades. (I also continued to take the pills every day.) I can report that I got so good at giving shots that I felt like a doctor on *ER*. It became second nature to puncture my ass—which finally became so numb that the whole process was as painful as wiping my nose.

Of course, my steroid use escalated as time went on, which just seemed . . . well, natural. I was a professional bodybuilder—everyone I knew was doing steroids, and no one considered it a big deal. I wasn't taking coke or crank or heroin; I wasn't hanging out in a dark alley doing drug deals. To my vast satisfaction, I learned that I could get steroids anywhere—the gym, a nightclub, a 7-11 parking lot, church, the bank, you name it. Back then, they weren't even expensive. For 100 Dianabol tablets, I paid $20—nowadays the same order would cost $300, and with them might come a warning about how they could be hazardous to your health. Back then no one said a word except, "You know where to get more."

And had anyone tried to convince me not to do them, I wouldn't have listened. Try telling a 19-year-old kid set on becoming a champion athlete that *anything* is dangerous to his health. Plus, I knew that something that made me feel this good couldn't possibly hurt me.

Sure, there were a few drawbacks besides my constant hunger. I noticed that I became increasingly angry, especially about the smallest things. The level of my rage actually scared me because I could easily go from a fun-loving, easygoing guy to an out-of-control, you-better-watch-your-back monster. This could happen in a nanosecond, because my hormones were on full tilt.

Yes, the formerly shy and sensitive Kenny became a bully who would fight anybody, anywhere, at any time. Compassion didn't matter to me—somehow the steroids messed with my mind and clouded the area that grants mercy to fellow human beings.

My victims grew in numbers when I took a night job as a bouncer at a nightclub to help pay the bills. I'd stand outside the joint (called "Satin's") with my chest puffed up, and I'd just wait for someone to mess with me. I'd drop a guy for any reason—such as looking at me funny.

I remember going into the bathroom in the club one night and noticing that a guy had missed the urinal and gotten a few drops of pee on the floor. Silently, I walked up to him, and in one lethal move, I kicked him hard in the backside.

"Whaaat are you doing, man?!" he screamed, now on his knees, gasping in pain.

I kicked him again, unconcerned with the fact that he had a big red welt on his butt now. I didn't care how pathetic he looked kneeling there with his pants around his ankles.

Another time, a guy threw his cigarette down on the nice carpeting in the club. I'm sure this happens at clubs all over the world, but it wasn't going to happen in mine.

"Pick it up, asshole!" I screamed at the man.

"Screw you, musclehead!" he said. He barely got the words out of his mouth before I dropped him cold, a few inches from his cigarette butt.

One of the worst incidents happened when I was with some friends at a bar called Tequila Pete's. Two big drunks were threatening to beat up another liquored-up lunatic who weighed in the neighborhood of 300 pounds. It was all tough talk, like these things usually are—but this testosterone-and-steroid-filled body-builder couldn't leave it alone.

The huge guy made the mistake of thinking I was one of his tormentors, so he stumbled up to me and said, "Hit me! Hit me, you loser!"

Any normal person would have just said to himself, *Oh, man, this dude is drunk. Just let it pass,* but I was already sizing up how I could beat him to a pulp. Quickly, I reasoned that I couldn't kick him in the head because he was much taller than my 5'11". I also figured that if I hit him in the stomach, he wouldn't feel it enough because he was so drunk. So I right-crossed him with all my strength, missed his face, and hit him smack in the center of his right ear.

He hit the ground face-first, and I walked away pleased, not even caring if the guy was still alive. Later on, I heard that this man was in a coma due to a blood clot in his head. To this day, I'm not sure if I was part of the cause—even all these years later, it still haunts me. Back then, of course, I had too many hormones raging in me to worry about doing ten years to life for manslaughter.

I *did* care about one thing a lot. If anyone said the word *nigger,* I'd drop him cold. I'd take the racist pig and pick him up by the hair, turn him upside down, and slam the top of his head into the floor. I was vicious, partly because of everything that had been stored up in me. That picked-on, small kid who had been abused was raging to get out and prove his point. With the help of steroids and my new body, I figured that I'd beat every feeling of inadequacy out of me, which now I know is an impossible dream. Still, I'd swing a fist for every person who'd ever hurt me in my life, not realizing that the person I was hurting the most with my rage was *myself.*

The scary thing is that my behavior was forgiven—it was even applauded as people started proclaiming that I was "one tough mutha." At the gym, everyone told me how great I looked and that I'd be a champion soon. I'd walk in, loving the moment when people would look at me during that first moment of the day, shake their heads, and say, "Man, it's like you just *look* at the barbells and you magically grow bigger and bigger."

Life got easier on all levels as I continued to take the steroids, which were now being given to me for free. I reasoned that I was feeding my body vitamins—really, really powerful ones.

Now would probably be a good time to tell you that I went from 140 to 170 pounds in a few weeks. Over the next several months, I kept going—until I was *300 pounds*. I felt as strong as an ox, and I wasn't afraid of anything. Even when I slept, I felt like Superman. Forget about starting my car in the morning . . . I figured I could just walk outside, pick up my car, and bench-press it a few times to get it going.

My new strength was exhilarating, and I continually tested how far I could push myself at the gym. Before I knew it, I could squat 600 pounds, bench-press 500, and curl 180 pounds—and I could do this while laughing. The entire time I worked out, I'd be grinning because the sheer lunacy of the situation was like the best joke I'd ever heard. Imagine this puny, 140-pound wussy-boy lifting 500 pounds—more than *three times* the weight of his former self! There's even a video of me cracking up while working out because it seemed so . . . well, *freaking unbelievable!*

Believe me, these days I *never* glorify steroids, and I'll get to the horror stories in a bit. But at that time, there was no way I could get to where I was weight-wise without those pills and shots. In fact, the quickest way I can explain the transformation is to say it was like a magician waving his wand and giving me the body of my dreams. I was so amazed that I'd wake up and stare at myself in the mirror, worried that those were someone else's muscles in the reflection. My shoulders looked as if they'd grown their *own* shoulders, and my biceps burst from my arms. My collarbone is narrow, which meant that I could only build so much width when it came to my upper body, yet I was exceeding my own expectations. My back looked like an earthquake had happened between my two shoulder blades, and what was carved out in its wake was something majestic, fierce, and stunning.

Understand that I didn't take any of this for granted, and I was in awe of every single part of me. However, my low self-esteem meant that I couldn't stand it when other people's jaws would drop and they'd say, "Wow, look at your body. You're the man!" Even their stares made me uncomfortable because I just couldn't take a compliment. My insecurities made me deflect their kind words by saying something nasty. It wasn't that I was mean; deep down, I was just so shy and nervous that I wanted to disappear.

"Get your skinny ass to the gym and you might fix that pathetic excuse for a body," I'd tell someone who had just said something nice to me. I wish I could take some of those cocky moments back because they mortify me now. These people were fans, and I turned on them like a pit bull. How I wish I could have been a role model for the kids in my neighborhood, but back then I could barely even get through the day without worrying about myself.

I wondered why the world wouldn't just leave me alone.

Chapter 7

Second Best Isn't Good Enough

At age 23, I was going nowhere and getting there fast. It was 1988, and old Officer Steroids was still unemployed due to police-department layoffs. Since I had no idea what to do, I started working out all the time to get ready for the local bodybuilding shows.

Sometimes I had a lot of competition at these events, while other times it would come down to me and one other guy in my weight class. In fact, that's how I met Rico McClinton. He was a bald, six-foot-tall guy who was the only other competitor in the light middleweight division at one show I entered. I actually defeated him and his 22-inch neck, which he used to swivel his head around and glare at me with disgust. He was so mad that I think he wanted to beat me up onstage. Let's just say that even though it was a local show, we were *loco* about being number one.

"I'll see you again," said Rico, almost as a warning.

"Count on it," I said, stifling the impulse to give him the finger while holding up my trophy.

And so went the life of a poor but proud aspiring athlete who was trying to build a life on runaway dreams. Then again, I wasn't really doing so badly. Levetta was working as a paralegal, and her modest income allowed us to pay all the bills. We lived in a tiny apartment with our own fridge, our own stove, and our own bug problems. But then money got really tight, and we were forced to move in with her parents. This, of course, made me feel terrible, because it was obvious I couldn't support my own wife—chalk it up to another way I failed.

To escape it all, I started working out all day. I'd get up in the morning and head to the gym, come home for lunch and a nap, and then go back to the gym in the evening. I didn't think of it like a career or anything; it was just something to do, *and* a handy way to escape Levetta, her parents, and all of our worries. I wasn't contemplating my next move as a bodybuilder—hell, I didn't even consider myself a pro. My small-town mentality didn't exactly figure that being a sports star was in the cards for me. Gas-station attendant, store manager, jailer—sure; pro athlete—please!

But fate has a strange way of intervening when you least expect it. Jeff Lawson, one of the biggest bodybuilding stars in Northern California, was living in Fresno that year, and he happened to work out at the gym I was practically living at in those days.

Jeff was nothing but an inspiration for me. "Flex, you could make a career out of bodybuilding," he said on one hot summer day, and I thought he'd lost his mind from the heat. But on the following day, he brought it up again. "I could help you—but only if you want," he suggested in a semi-pushy way.

I grumbled something, and that night, I drove home thinking, *Why would anyone want to help me? I'm not worth it.*

Slowly, Jeff just assumed that he was helping me, and I didn't have the nerve to tell him to hit the road. He told me that we weren't just training for the thrill of it or as a way to pass the time. He was going to get me ready for some serious competitions.

"Yeah, but Jeff, I don't know if I can—"

"Yes, you *can,*" he interrupted.

And so, at the end of May 1988, I stood backstage at the Russ Warner Competition in Northern California with 170 other men—who I just knew were bigger, stronger, and better than I was. My pessimism started to rear its ugly head, but I went out there and did my best. I did the standard poses—the double bicep that's so identifiable, the lat spread that showed the expansion of my lats from both front and rear. Thankfully, no one could see my nervousness or that I walked onstage with my fists balled up as if I were ready to fight.

"And the winner is . . . Flex Wheeler!" the announcer exclaimed.

I won my class, although I couldn't quite believe it. I figured that the judges had made a mistake.

While I was just staring at my trophy, Jeff came over and hugged me tightly. "There's only one person who needs to believe in you a little bit more, Ken. That person is you," he said, holding my right hand up in a victory pose while the newspaper photographers blinded us with flashbulbs.

That was the first major show that I won as a middleweight, and the following year I took first place at two bigger California bodybuilding contests—the Contra Costa Competition and the Governor's Cup. I was flying, man! I wish I could tell you that from that point on, it was a cakewalk, but I was still worried about winning the upcoming California State Championship. In fact, my worries could have easily become a self-fulfilling type of defeat, because when you keep telling yourself that you'll lose, then chances are your worst fears will come true. I don't know if you've ever noticed this, but if you put all that negative energy out there, the universe has a way of stirring up that turmoil and slamming it back in your face—hard.

What's funny is that even after these wins, I was really depressed because I figured that they were just flukes. So I came home and went into an even more complete, full-on training mode. Even though everyone around me thought I could compete on a national level, I felt it was a long shot at best.

The big problem was that I was uneducated when it came to the laws of the body—especially the basic principles of nutrition. At the time, all I ate was tuna fish out of the can and hunks of sourdough bread that I ripped off in fistfuls before slamming them down my throat. In addition, I drank tons of sports drinks, which just pumped all sorts of sugar and empty calories into my system. Basically, I didn't know how to diet, so I downed things without thinking. As for exercise, it was all lifting and no cardio: I'd work on a certain body part until I exhausted the muscle, to the point where it could have torn permanently. I simply didn't know any better . . . but luckily for me, the results were miraculously good. I had no fat on me, which is why I didn't need cardio to melt off the lard. At the time I was competing, my 300 steroid-induced pounds were mostly pure muscle.

I felt good, despite the fact that I wasn't really sleeping at all. My mind was simply too active and so was my stomach, which would growl so loudly in the middle of the night that it was like sleeping with a pack of wolves. During the day I'd be so exhausted that I'd catch a nap or two; and then at night I'd walk around in the dark with every single worry in my life playing out like some sort of late-night horror movie that I couldn't turn off: *Will I ever have any money? Will I ever be able to take care of Levetta and our baby?* (Oh, did I forget to mention that Levetta was pregnant?) *Will I become a good person? Will I ever eat pizza again? Is my car going to be repossessed? Is Levetta going to leave me? Will the baby be healthy? Was that a cockroach I just saw?*

As the California Bodybuilding Championship approached, a new slew of worries played on my mind's movie screen. The truth was that I was clueless when it came to the whole bodybuilding game. For starters, I didn't recognize the sheer enormity of the show I was about to do, and I was naïve about what it meant when it came to my future. Plus, I was in awe when I looked at the other guys, which made it difficult for me to talk to them. So I got a reputation for being a rude new upstart—even though I was so intimidated by them that I couldn't say a word.

I *did* learn how the money part worked. Amateur bodybuilders basically make jack—the cash comes when you qualify to be a pro. Pros get a slew of endorsement deals; and they get to be signed by Joe Weider, who owns his own bodybuilding empire, including almost all the magazines devoted to the sport that you see on the newsstands. Before the deals and before Joe looks your way, it's like being the best high school football player: You get the glory, but you still have to ask your mom (or wife) for an allowance. When you get to the next level, you get the spoils. The sad fact is that most people trip up between the two levels, never to be heard from again. Your job is not to trip, and that's not easy when the rug under you keeps moving.

Finally, the big day arrived. "WELCOME TO THE CALIFORNIA BODYBUILDING CHAMPIONSHIP—1989" read the big banner outside the San Diego Sports Arena. I didn't feel very welcome because my trainer, Jeff Lawson, wasn't able to go due to obligations to his business, and Levetta had just given birth to our son, Kennen. However, my gym paid for me to go to San Diego, which was very cool, because I certainly couldn't pay for it myself. Then some friends from Fresno came down, and just seeing their smiling, proud faces gave me an energy boost that couldn't be found anywhere else. It got me through the pre-judging in the morning, where I did the mandatory poses again. This was also where I got all the instructions about the competition and the rules.

For this competition, I was competing in the light-heavyweight division. That night I was back onstage doing my posing routine to music. I did the most common poses again—the double bicep, the front pose, the lat spread, the side press. Easy stuff. As I watched the other guys pose, I thought that I could quite possibly win. Nah, what was I thinking? *No way. I really didn't do that well, and I don't know anything about bodybuilding. I'm certainly not worthy of a trophy.*

"And the number-one bodybuilder in the light-heavyweight division in the state of California is Flex Wheeler!" shouted the judge. To my amazement, he continued on, telling the world: "Flex has also won the overall championship tonight!"

My heart stopped for a minute because a winner was in the house and . . . it was me! The auditorium went wild, but in my mind, things were very quiet. I won, which meant that I *did* do well and I *was* worthy. The following minutes were a blur.

"Flex, how does it feel to be the best bodybuilder in the state of California?" asked one of several reporters who were circling me like they wanted to either adopt me or mug me.

How does it feel? That should have been obvious because I was crying. "Wow," I said, "I don't really know what this means, but it, uh, it feels really good to say that I've won something."

I looked for my friends, but I'd lost them in the crowd. My view was blocked by the other bodybuilders, disappointed mammoth men who were suddenly shaking my hand and slapping me on the shoulders because it was the thing to do. "Way to go, Flex," one of my co-competitors said, and I was in shock. He appeared to be truly happy for me, and for the first time, I was pleased to be up there with the other athletes. I was proud to be a part of this sport.

These thoughts were fleeting, however, because basic shock set back in. *Maybe they made a mistake,* I worried, as my insides twisted into a knot. But it was for real; and to prove it, I was handed a trophy—a golden, life-sized Excalibur sword, which really freaked me out because it was huge, heavy, and quite beautiful.

"Excuse us, Flex." One of the public relations women from the competition broke my reverie. "The crew from ESPN wants to interview you," she said.

I had no idea what that meant, so I just trailed after her. "You mean, ESPN like the TV network?" I whispered to her.

"Exactly like the TV network," she whispered back with a smile.

"Can I call my wife really quick and tell her what just happened?" I asked, wondering if I had the change to make a call.

"Sure, call anyone you want," she said.

I began to think that being a winner did have its perks. I didn't even have to put change in the phone backstage—it was free. My first call was to Levetta, who answered the phone on the first ring. "How's the baby? Did he eat?" I immediately asked.

She never answered my questions; instead she cried, "Kenny, what happened? Did you win?"

"Oh yeah, I did," I said, smiling from ear to ear, as she screamed so loudly that I thought my eardrum had shattered.

We didn't have too much time for chitchat because that ESPN camera crew was ready for me. Now, this was too cool—I watched ESPN all the time, and never for one minute did I think I'd ever be on TV. The only problem was that after the reporter sprayed his hair for 15 minutes and put all sorts of powder on his face, he had to interview someone inexperienced when it came to giving good sound bites. Basically, I just stood there in front of the camera hoping to look normal. I certainly didn't want to jump up and down and come off as some idiot. Yet in my quest to look smart and regular, I didn't appear to be as excited, and the reporter was upset with me. It didn't help that I didn't know what to say, so I answered all of his inquiries with a quick and emotionless "Yes" or "No."

No, I didn't know what the future held for me as a bodybuilder. Yes, I spent a lot of time in the gym. No, I didn't think I'd win. Yes, I was happy (although I had the most serious look on my face, as if I were about to have brain surgery). Yes, I just wanted to go home . . . and so on.

"Can I say hi to my grandmother?" I asked the reporter, who nodded. "Hi, Grandmommy! I won," I said, staring directly into the camera with a dopey look on my face. "I'll see you soon."

A day later I was back in Fresno, where I ended up on the local news—and thus ended my first brush with major celebrity.

"Baby, I knew you could do it. I always told them that I expected great things from you," said my biggest fan (Grandmommy).

Two days after the competition, I was back in the gym. The bodybuilding gig basically means that you're always getting ready for the next show. The only difference at this point was that someone might come up every once in a while to ask for my autograph. All in all, I found that winning wasn't that fantastic a deal, except that my grandmother was really proud of me. I even let her keep the Excalibur sword for a couple of months, and she showed it to every little old lady in Fresno—and those gray gals always asked to hold the thing. At the very least, I hoped it kept the muggers away.

A few weeks later, I was asked to compete in the Nationals, the biggest bodybuilding competition held each year. I was scared to death at the thought of this show, so I became an even bigger pessimist. I'd stare into the mirror and pick every single body part to shreds. *This needs work,* I'd tell myself. *That's weak. You'll never win Nationals with those legs, and they'll laugh you off the stage with those arms.* When other people told me that I had a good shot, I'd give myself a wake-up call: *What do they know? They're just flapping their gums.*

The 1989 Nationals were held in Miami, and the heat was on, so to speak. For once in my life, I was actually happy to be somewhere new, and something odd happened the moment I walked into the First National Bank Arena. I felt a chill that had nothing to do with the air-conditioning—there was also an overwhelming, cold feeling of kill-or-be-killed backstage between the bodybuilders stalking these grounds. Yes, each of us knew that luck and hard work got us to this moment, but there could only be one winner. Each stone face said that this was no lovefest—it was war. I was up for the battle, and I screwed on my intense, take-no-prisoners game face. But when no one was looking, I allowed myself one minute to feel the giddy rush that came from knowing that I was at Nationals for the first time. Getting here meant that I was one of the best bodybuilders in the nation.

Something else was going on inside of me that seemed to indicate that I'd been abducted by aliens and replaced with another Flex Wheeler. You see, for the first time, I thought I would win. Well, I thought it for a minute, but hey, it was progress. Of course, the second I saw some of the advanced competitors stroll in with their posses, my hopes went down, down, down. *You're gonna lose!* my mind screamed, and the breath in my lungs became heavy. Disappointed and frustrated, I glared at the top guys, and then I glanced at the 30,000 seats that were already sold out. All the old doubts came flooding back. *What am I doing here? Can I perform in front of an audience this big? Am I even in the league of some of these men?* The answers were easy: I was there because I was crazy; I would freeze in front of the crowd; and no way was I in the league of these other men. End of story.

A few crank phone calls to my hotel room confirmed all that self-doubt, and even wrapped a bow around it. When the phone rang at 2 A.M., I thought it might be Levetta calling about the baby, so my heart rate instantly sped up as I reached for the receiver.

"I'm gonna beat you because you're crap!" said the husky tone of a man on the other end.

"Who the hell is this?" my sleep-thickened voice intoned into the plastic.

"You suck," said the voice.

Sitting up in a ball of fury, I replied, "You have my room number? You want to come up here and settle it? Why wait 'til we're on stage? I'll kick your ass right now!" I'll never be sure which one of the other bodybuilders put some friend of his up to call me and psych me out—but this was backstage backstabbing at its worst.

The line went dead, but I was so pissed that falling asleep wasn't an option. I felt like I was being squeezed hard from all directions— I couldn't sleep, I couldn't eat, and I couldn't win.

Competition day rolled around, and my nerves were rocking so hard that I thought I was having an out-of-body experience. The one consolation is that once I stepped out onstage, I was blinded by the spotlights, so I couldn't see the audience. I could only glance out as far as the second row, which is where I spotted some stern-looking observers giving me attitude. Obviously, they could see that I was just a kid from Fresno with a new baby, no job, and a big dream that just wasn't going to come true. A little bit of stage fright entered my system. This wasn't exactly a little thing that I could shake off—at the Nationals, every reaction at every moment is the difference between going home a winner or a man with regrets.

Somehow I got through the mandatory set of poses, and then I was told to wait for my next call. Backstage, a psych-you-out house party was in action, and I was ready to dance. As witnessed by my "wake-up call," the largest men in the world can play equally sizable head games. Their stares and glares spoke volumes, but I gave what I got by looking back with eyes of fury. I really didn't blame the other bodybuilders, because there was so much money on the line. Whoever won at Nationals would wave good-bye to their amateur days forever—two seconds after getting that trophy, he'd turn pro and watch the cash pour in.

Jeff had a team of people training me now, and they told me on the QT that there's an unofficial law in professional bodybuilding: "If you're at Nationals three times and you keep losing, you'll never get a shot. You're branded a loser, and it's basically over."

The only thing keeping me going that day was that this was my first shot, and I could keep going. Unfortunately, I didn't walk away the winner. It's funny—a few moments before the end of competition, contenders know with about 90-percent accuracy where they rank because the scores are called out after each pose. This means that it rarely happens that the overall winner is a total shock.

When I'm in a competition, my mind becomes a human computer, running the numbers again and again. (I wish I'd been this good at math in school.) The worst moments would be when I was sure someone else had won, yet I'd try to figure out a way that my first conclusion was wrong. It's never—I repeat, never—wrong.

My gut ached when I tallied up the score at that first Nationals, because even before the judges announced it, I knew I was walking away in fifth place. I was a loser in my mind because only the person with the number-one ranking was the winner—at least in my book.

"You did so well, Flex," my trainers said, proceeding to give me a quick laundry list of my weaknesses.

I couldn't bear to hear it, so I tuned them out. However, in my despair, a few good things happened. I was really impressed when, after the competition, several veteran bodybuilders came up to me to give me some constructive criticism. I was shocked that they would even take the time to talk to me as if I were one of their own. For instance, Cory Everson, a building legend who's now a commentator on ESPN, said a lot of nice things about my routine and my look.

Laura Creavalle, a pro builder, pointed out that I was really small for my class, and I should work on my legs. "Basically, they judge you on your body, your balance, how you groom yourself, your look, how you carry yourself, your poses, your presentation, and your attitude," she reminded me. "When it's close between you and someone else, even the slightest thing can make you lose." She insisted that "the mark of a true champion is when you take care of everything and don't leave even one stone unturned."

It was good advice, although I was too distraught to hear it or take it to heart.

Before I left Miami, I took a long, hard look at the other guys for the last time. I saw men whose faces were on the cover of sports magazines, and I saw mugs that were on TV all the time. I knew that these men had paid their dues; they'd been here before, and that shouldn't have intimidated me. Still, I felt beneath them, and I knew that I needed to find some way to rise to their level.

"Let's line up the winners for a group shot," a cheery public relations person suggested. "Flex, we need you," she chirped, and it suddenly dawned on me that I *did* take fifth, so I stood with the other champs. Maybe it was good, but it wasn't good enough for me.

When I got home, I had a few serious decisions to make about what I'd finally decided was my career. The deal is that if you've competed at Nationals, then you should only continue to do national shows. Why take a step back into less-significant territory? I shocked everybody when I chose not to do Nationals again, but instead tried a junior national show. Frankly, I wasn't ready for another Nationals, and I couldn't handle another loss. At the Junior Nationals in 1990, I took second place, which seemed like an improvement, but I was more upset than ever because I thought I'd definitely win that one.

Next came the USA Championship in 1991. Even though it was a pro competition, amateurs could participate in it as a way to qualify for the pro-division Nationals later that year. I took second again, and I felt like I'd been run over by a cement truck—I couldn't turn pro by being second. Even worse was the fact that I lost first place by *one point.*

One lousy point! One look. One fraction-of-an-inch movement. One second where I moved my body in the wrong direction. One freaking mistake. It hurt like hell. Whether you lose by ten million points or just one doesn't matter—it's the same empty feeling. Each time I looked at my second-place trophy, I felt like I was in *last* place. Remember that I've always been self-destructive, which in a sick way is actually a bit helpful at times. That trait has made me want to push back even more.

This time, however, *life* shoved back even harder. After the USA Championship, I was extremely broke, and Levetta was a little sick of the lifestyle I was keeping her and the baby in. "Kenny, we need to make some changes here if this little family is going to survive," she said, and I knew that she had a point. Soon it was going to be time to leave bodybuilding forever, get a job somewhere, and just pay the bills. It wasn't fun or fair, but it was common sense.

Strangely, the loss of my dream bothered me more than I thought it would. Each time I thought about quitting, I'd shake my head and think, *But what if? What if I did just one more show? What if I won?* Then I'd shake myself out of it, realizing that my "what if" days were about over.

But no, my dreaming days weren't over—my marriage, however, was. Levetta and I decided to divorce. The sad truth was that we got hitched as kids who had no clue about adult life. Flashing through my mind was my younger self reminding Levetta that we had no business getting married at ages 19 (me) and 20 (her). For once, I wasn't happy to be right, but the bottom line was that we simply grew apart, and our needs were on the opposite ends of the spectrum. She wanted a stable family life, including a "normal" husband who worked 9 to 5, and I wanted to follow some shadowy dream into the unknown. The two worlds couldn't mix, so we split up with her getting custody of Kennen, while I had liberal visitation rights.

What followed was one of the most depressing times in my life. I moved from Fresno to Los Angeles and started working as a rent-a-cop just to survive. Yet I still couldn't pay my bills; my lousy, dented-up Toyota Corolla was in danger of being repossessed; and I barely had enough money for the apartment I was sharing with my friend George. I was two steps away from being homeless.

The bright spot in my life was the famed Gold's Gym in Venice, where world-class athletes and movie stars work out. Just like the day I wandered into the karate studio as a kid wanting to take lessons, I entered the doors of Gold's Gym knowing that I couldn't afford the steep monthly fee. But thanks to my TV exposure, the management saw fit to offer me a deal I couldn't refuse: "What if we let you train here for the bargain-basement price of free?"

I couldn't believe my luck, or the company sweating around me. On certain days, Magic Johnson would be to my right on one of the machines, and Wesley Snipes would be on my left. I also made some new friends, including one unlikely candidate: Rico, the guy I'd beaten a few years back in Fresno.

"I told you we'd meet up again," he said, holding out a hand. Neither of us were the guys we used to be back then; we'd graduated to the status of grown men with something in common—the highs and lows of pro bodybuilding. That handshake was the beginning of a life-long friendship.

Around the same time, I started getting a ton of fan mail, especially after ESPN aired my year-old "interview" from the California Bodybuilding Championship about 1,000 times. It was such a positive thing because I couldn't believe that people not only sent their good wishes, they'd send money with a note saying, "Here's 20 bucks. Have dinner on me." I can't tell you how much I appreciated these gifts—believe it or not, I lived off that money. One day a crispy $100 bill fell at my feet, and I almost wept. Now I could finally buy some lunch meat from the deli and pay the electric bill. In all of my life, I'd never heard of people sending money through the mail—I thought it was cuckoo, but I was really thankful. Of course, when my almost-repossessed car was actually stolen, I gave in and felt desperate again—but I was able to depend on the kindness of strangers. At the gym, people started giving me rides and bringing me meals, figuring that that was the only way I'd get around or eat that day. Rico, who had become my training partner, also paid for many of my breakfasts or dinners, and I don't know what I would have done without his open heart and equally open wallet.

Life finally gave me a real break when a sports legend named Charles Glass began to train me. The man who trained Magic Johnson and Wesley Snipes pushed me hard, and I performed. He was pleased with my progress and agreed to train me for free.

Inside, I still felt worthless most days because I didn't have a real job and didn't even consider myself an athlete. At least Levetta was nice about letting me see Kennen; she didn't even make me pay child support at the time because she knew I could barely support myself. You see, deep down she did love me and was very hurt by our split, but she just couldn't take my lifestyle.

I used the little money I had to come to Fresno on weekends, stay with Grandmommy, and visit my little boy. One day I took Kennen to the local fair, and guess who we ran into? My daughter, Brandy, and her mother, Medusa, who was trailing closely behind. I couldn't believe that Brandy was a big girl now—I quickly calculated that she was about 12—but sadly, she didn't even know her father well enough to pick me out of a crowd. Frankly, I didn't know how to act, and above all, I didn't want to get into a knock-down, drag-out fight with Medusa in front of the kids. I thought about just admiring Brandy from across the field, but that plan was nixed when Medusa spotted me and whispered to Brandy, who shyly approached Kennen and me.

"Hi, honey," I said to Brandy, "You're so beautiful. In fact, would you mind if the three of us took a picture together?"

The shy, willowy girl gave me the same smile I'd seen at the car wash when she was a little girl. With some trepidation, she even put her hand on Kennen's tiny shoulder, which made me want to cry.

At that point, Medusa sprang into action and started screaming, "You ain't gonna take a make-believe picture and pretend to be a family!" She snatched Brandy by the arm and pulled her away.

"Daddy, who was that girl?" Kennen asked when they were gone. Since I was so sick of the lies and hostility, I answered him honestly. "That's your sister," I said.

A few weeks later, I called Brandy, and she talked to me for about five minutes. The girl had a lot of hate in her heart about why I hadn't accepted her when she was a baby.

I understood and just listened to her. Finally, I chuckled and said, "I guess your mom told you a couple of bad things about me."

"A couple! Try a million!" said Brandy, and both of us burst out laughing.

It was a tiny step, but it also marked the beginning of my becoming her father in every sense of the word. In fact, this experience was enough to make me call my own father. I realized that I didn't harbor any hate in my heart for a man who, like myself, wasn't born perfect.

"Kenny, is that you? I'm so glad to hear from you," said the scratchy voice on the other end of the phone. "How are you, son?"

"Daddy, let me tell you what's been going on," I said.

⊙—⊙

In 1992, I chose to compete at the USA Competition again. I pretty much figured that this was my last chance at bodybuilding as a career, so I was prepared to compete in one more big show and then go back to being a cop. At least one day I'd be able to tell Kennen that Daddy tried to do something really big once upon a time.

The competition was intense from the moment I walked through the steel backstage doors and was met by laser-eyed competitors who essentially hated my well-toned guts. We all sized each other up for what seemed like forever, until an official came in and said, "It's show time, gentlemen."

Then, to use one of my favorite expressions, it was on like Donkey Kong. The lights went up, we hit the stage, and I almost melted because the spotlights made it about 110 degrees up there. We're talking 21 over-sized men in an enclosed space with very little oxygen. It was emotionally and physically draining before the competition even began.

Most of the time when I'm onstage, I run on pure disgust with myself. I'm almost in a daze, to the point that people think I'm arrogant or cocky. The truth is, I'm so emotional that I'm afraid I might lose it. I just keep telling myself, *Keep it together, keep it together.*

That wasn't easy advice at the USA Competition, since the crowd numbered 40,000, and the event was airing live on ESPN. At age 27, I felt like an old man when it came to this sport that I loved, a sport that never seemed to embrace me quite as hard as I embraced it. But knowing that I had nothing to lose, I just went for it. At the end, I did a mental tally in my head; then I added it up again—and again. *Sweet Jesus, that can't be right!* I thought.

I had a perfect score.

"The winner is Flex Wheeler!" said the announcer, and the crowd erupted into cheers so loud that the floor shook.

I had arrived. But emotionally, little Kenny Wheeler from Fresno was having a breakdown. Tears flooded my eyes, and when the huge gold trophy was placed in my hands, I fell to my knees, draped my body over the statue, and began openly sobbing. Men I didn't know were patting me on the back and insisting that I stand up because all this wailing was unnerving them.

Meanwhile, Joe Weider—the "Godfather" of this sport—leaned over and whispered in my ear, "Don't worry, Flex. I'll take care of you. I'm putting you under contract."

I just couldn't believe it. This had been my last chance—I was Cinderella after midnight struck, and yet I'd still lucked out. And the highs just kept on coming. I looked into the audience and saw the face of a man who had never seen me in any competition . . . my father, who also had tears in his eyes.

Next, it was time to party! Since I was a pro now and the deals were coming in, I decided to buy myself a red Corvette, which was my dream car as a boy. I hired Charles Glass as my official trainer (paying him for the first time in three years), took Rico out for a great dinner, and did my first magazine cover for Joe. The headline read: "FLEX WHEELER MAKES THE PROS." Every single time I saw that damn thing on a newsstand, my body went into an involuntary shudder.

Remember how I said that I was always perceived as a cocky, arrogant bastard? Well, I couldn't help but take the first steps of becoming one for real. Yes, now I had a few dollars and, therefore, I thought I was all that. Joe was paying me $3,500 a month, but I acted like it was a million.

The last bits of Kenny did surface when I returned home, however. Sitting in that little house in Fresno, it was Kenny who insisted that now it was time to pay his grandmother back and help with a few bills and food. "You can retire now, Grandmommy," I said. "Let me do this for you. Let me take care of you."

The woman who began working in 1922 could finally put her feet up and stop cleaning up other people's messes, but she wouldn't hear of it. "You don't stop until death catches you, baby," she said.

Little did I know that death wasn't on her tail—it was on mine.

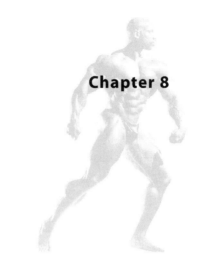

Chapter 8

Love and Loss

Happiness sometimes comes in waves, and I knew that the one I was riding after my win in 1992 couldn't last forever. Or could it? Charles and Rico claimed that I was progressing nicely in my training—I was lifting 500 pounds and was squatting almost 700. Occasionally I'd cough up blood because of the pressure this put on my lungs, but I just swallowed it back down. I was still taking my steroids, and no one thought much about it. I'd give myself shots in the morning, brush my teeth, and drive to the gym where other members would high-five me the minute I walked through the door.

However, for the first time in my career, I did begin to worry about my body. What if I ripped or strained a muscle and it put me out of commission? Charles and Rico knew my limitations and my strengths, so they made sure that I didn't push too hard.

When Charles thought that I couldn't push it another inch, he'd say, "Take a break. I mean it, man! Rest now." On other days when I was dragging because my worries had kept me up all night, he'd say, "We're going to do 30 more reps." I'd give him a disgusted look. "Make that *50*. Let's go!" he'd retort, making it clear who was in charge.

I got used to the physical pain, which actually became the least of my worries. Bodybuilding is much more a psychological game than most people imagine—of course, you need mass to move the weight, but you can't move anything if you're not in sync mentally. That's why Gold's Gym suddenly became a very serious place. There were times when no one spoke, the music was shut off, and I could almost hear my muscles moving inch by inch. When regular old people came in and started to bug me, they were told to pack up their gear and hit the road, for this was no laughing matter. This was life and death to us—one screwup could end my career, which at that time was my entire life.

As for the pain, I'd often lift the weight bar and feel a small muscle fiber begin to tear. That's when I'd have to stop and let it heal up. The danger would be if I *didn't* feel the muscle tearing, because that kind of thing could have kept me out of the gym for months. It's a fine line between pushing . . . and pushing too hard. Too hard says that a muscle has detached from the bone, which means extreme pain and internal bleeding. Let me tell you that a bruise on the inside of a muscle is the worst—it hurts so bad that you want to cry for your mama.

Even worse is tearing a pectoral muscle, because you can see the injury deteriorate by the minute. The little nook under the armpit fills up with dark red blood until a pouch hangs down, and the pain is excruciating. The first time I tore a pec muscle, I heard it before I felt it: *riiiiiipppp*. I also tore my left bicep—when that happened, my arm made a loud "*psssssst*" sound, like my body was hissing. It's the most horrible noise in the whole world. And once I squatted to lift about 500 pounds and almost tore my hamstring muscle. In fact, a few more injured muscle fibers down there would have meant that my career would have been over, or I might never have walked again without crutches—but my mind was so wrapped around being a world-class champion that I wasn't sure which of those two would have been the worse fate.

The nights were the hardest, because I needed some companionship when I couldn't sleep (which was often). It wasn't that I just wanted to get laid; I mostly just craved a warm and friendly voice or a soft shoulder. I tried dating, but many girls didn't understand why I couldn't wine and dine them—wining and dining wasn't on my diet.

The ladies also didn't get why I wasn't lavishing them with expensive gifts. Sure, I was a champion athlete, but champion dollars weren't at my fingertips because I was paying off some debts and finally helping to support my son.

By the time 1993 rolled around, I was dating a real pain, a woman we'll call "Hedy" because she had some pretty heady dreams about being the wife of a sports superstar. I wasn't in love with her, so I really didn't want her around later in the year when I went to observe the Nationals in Long Beach, California.

The first day I was there, I ran into one of the judges, a muscular powerlifter named Paul Love. He was accompanied by his lovely twin daughters, Liz and Madeline. Did I mention that they were beautiful, gorgeous, breathtaking? Well, you get the idea.

Madeline Love. Her name said it all, because for me it was love at first sight. I'd never experienced this sort of feeling before. The moment I saw her, something strange happened—I didn't want to rip off her clothes or impress her with my trophies or bodybuilding stats. I saw her and wanted to cry.

She had long, dark hair, soft brown eyes, and was thin, but not frail, at about 98 pounds. She was wearing faded blue jeans and a T-shirt, but it might as well have been a ball gown to me. Her beauty was astonishing, which is why I couldn't help but stare at her in the hotel lobby, all the while wondering, *What kind of man do you have to be to have someone that beautiful want to be with you? God, I wish I was that type of man.*

Of course, I didn't say any of this to Madeline. I just stared at her while keeping my lips zipped. But as soon as she walked away, I became Flex Bond, a superspy in search of details about Madeline Love's life. I found out that she was single and lived in San Jose, which was about 300 miles from L.A.—but what was spending a few hours in the car on clogged freeways when it came to true love?

Madeline knew all about bodybuilding because her father had been a competitor and judge for years. I was too chicken to approach her that night, but a few months later, fate intervened. Paul Love called and asked me to do a guest appearance at a show he was judging in San Jose. I jumped at the opportunity.

"Flex, thanks so much for doing the show. If it's okay with you, I'll have my daughter Madeline pick you up at the airport," Paul mentioned while we made plans for my visit.

"Oh, Madeline . . . your really cute daughter?"

Paul could only laugh. "She's a twin, Flex. They're both cute," he said.

I ignored his little jab and said, "Madeline doesn't have to pick me up. I can get a cab."

"No, my daughters always help me out," Paul insisted in his firm but polite way.

"Look, this isn't a good idea," I suddenly blurted out.

Paul could only reply, "Why is that, Flex? Why can't my daughter pick you up at the airport?"

Since I couldn't say that I was totally infatuated with her, I just replied, "Look, Paul. Keep your daughter away from me."

Paul snickered and said that he'd pick me up himself.

The minute I saw Paul at the airport, I had only one question for him: "So where's Madeline?"

He smiled and rolled his eyes. "She'll be at the show tonight— if that's okay with you." Then he leaned closer and added, "Flex, do you like Madeline or something?"

"Yes, I do, sir," I said. "But you and I are the only ones who know."

He walked away chuckling like this wasn't the first time some dope had had a crush on one of his girls.

That night at the show, I ran into Paul's other daughter, Liz, who was pregnant. "Where's your sister?" I asked in a tone that was a bit too serious.

"Oh, she's around," said Liz with a grin. She was obviously in on the secret, too.

"Do me a favor," I said, tossing off my best cool-dude look. "Tell your sister that I'm in love with her."

To which Liz sweetly replied, "Hey, Flex?"

"What?"

"Do it yourself!" she said, turning around and waddling away from me. I had to admit that these girls were nobody's fools.

In the hotel lobby, I started to rip myself apart. It had been stupid of me to say that to Liz. I was a real jerkoff who thought he was God's gift to women, which certainly wasn't true. Like an old home movie being clicked on, images of my father's girlfriend molesting me came back. I wondered if I was messed up forever when it came to love, relationships, and sex. Was I broken beyond repair in this department? Yes, the plentiful groupies were so sexual toward me, but these weren't the kind of women I wanted to be around for the long term. I wanted someone good and whole . . . like Madeline.

Of course, once I got to the competition, the cocky part of me tried to shove these thoughts away. I stood backstage and thought, *I'm a pro athlete, damn it! I can get any tail I want. Who needs these other complications? This relationship stuff never seems to work out anyway. I don't have time for a new girlfriend with all her stupid demands and—*

"Hi, I'm Madeline. Remember me?" a feminine voice asked, interrupting my pessimistic reverie.

Again, I took one look at the hair, the eyes, and the smile, and I wanted to melt at Madeline's feet. I wanted to just hold her in my arms, but instead I said, "Oh, yeah. I sort of remember you."

There wasn't much time to chat, because three of her girlfriends were surrounding her like armed bodyguards. They looked only too ready to kick my ass if I bothered their homegirl.

"Are you going to watch me pose?" I asked Madeline, ignoring the searing looks on her friends' faces.

"Sure," she said.

"I'd like to talk to you later if that's okay," I bravely announced. If she would have told me no, I'm not sure where I'd be today, but luck was on my side.

"Later, fine," she said. Two little words and my future was foolproof, although I didn't know it at the time.

After the show, Madeline lived up to her word. She sat down next to me backstage to talk about the other bodybuilders, the weather, movies, and so on. She was very nice, and so fine-looking that I wasn't myself. I was in awe. Finally, I blurted out the question that had been burning in my mind: "Do you have a boyfriend?"

"Yes, I do," she replied.

Looking her straight in the eye, I said, "Dump him." She didn't answer, so I continued on. "Dump him for me."

For a second I thought that I was winning points with the no-nonsense, direct approach, and then Madeline narrowed those gorgeous eyes of hers. "Why would I do that?" she demanded. "Who the hell are *you*? And why do you act the way you do?"

I didn't answer that. Instead, I dug myself into an even deeper hole. "This boyfriend," I said, practically spitting the words out, "can't do anything for you like I can."

By now, Madeline had obviously grown tired of my act. She kind of smirked and said, "I don't think so."

Yet I kept going. "I'll fly you first-class to L.A. and take care of you. Everything will be first rate," I tossed out.

"You know what, Flex?" Madeline said, standing up abruptly and folding her hands across her chest. (Inside, I winced, 'cause this wasn't going to be good.) "All that stuff," she continued, "doesn't mean anything to me. I'm not that type of girl, and I won't quit my boyfriend for some conceited bodybuilder. Can I go now?"

Obviously, I'd dug myself to the center of the Earth. "Yes, you can go," I said, arrogantly. Then to rescue the situation I'd clearly blown, I asked in the most humble tone, "Miss Love, what are you doing tonight?"

Shockingly, she didn't punch me! "I'm going out with my girlfriends."

"Can I go—with all of you?" I asked.

At this point, I saw a glimmer in her eyes that said she at least found me amusing. "Yes, you can come with all of us," she said, emphasis on *all* and *us,* as in *there will be a posse.*

"But I want to be *your* special guest," I insisted.

Worn out by now, she sighed and replied, "Fine! All right! You're my special guest."

Later we all went out to a club, and I found out that the love of my life also had a brother named Wayland who had a special request for me. "Hey, Flex, can you keep my sister real busy? I want to hang out with her friends," he begged.

Immediately I loved this guy. His request was certainly fine with me . . . but Madeline ended up ignoring me. I was so mad that I sat in a funk until the next emotion came over me, which was rage. I soon found out that Madeline's boyfriend had called her and found out about her "special guest." The bastard was reportedly on his way to the club to take care of the situation.

What I didn't know was that a few weeks earlier, Madeline's boyfriend had been flipping through a bodybuilding magazine when he found an article on me. "Do you think this guy's good-looking?" he asked Madeline.

Unfortunately, she did the worst thing possible for a guy's fragile ego: She didn't say anything for a really long time. Then she finally said, "Well, yes, Flex is actually very handsome."

That comment pissed off her boyfriend to the point that he was going to make sure I wasn't that handsome anymore (as if he had that power). Well, I didn't need that kind of publicity, so I thought, *Forget her. I hate her.* I snuck out and went home without even saying good night.

A few months later, I did a guest-posing session at the California State Championship (the show I'd won in 1989). In 1993, the competition was held in my hometown of Fresno. It felt as if I'd come full circle. Rico and I drove to the show in my new Mercedes SL500, which I'd bought thanks to an endorsement deal. It was the first time a Wheeler had owned a Mercedes, so I drove to the show at about 150 miles per hour.

Rico was beside himself. "Can you slow down, Flex?" he implored. "I'd like to live."

I was having a ball. "We're tearing this town down tonight," I told him. All I knew was that this was my city, and I was the highest-ranking bodybuilder in town. I'd won the USA Champion in 1992, had come in number one at the Ironman Pro in 1993, and had gotten another first-place trophy at the Arnold Classic. And tons of women wanted to hang out with me. *Madeline who?* I thought. *Why should I let one girl who doesn't even live near me break me down and make me feel like nothing?*

When we got into town, I insisted that we go down to the Marriott hotel to check out the bar and the honeys. As soon as we got there, the elevator opened, and out waltzed Paul Love with the biggest honey of all time—Madeline.

"Let's go, Rico," I said, turning my back on her, although I could feel her eyes drilling into my skull.

"What the hell?!" Rico exclaimed. "We just got here!"

Remember, I'd known Rico long enough so that all it took for him to understand was one look at my face. "Who *is* that broad?" he asked.

"No one," I mumbled. "I can't stand her."

By now, Madeline had quickly moved back into the elevator and was on her way up to her room.

"Hey, Dawg," Rico said, staring at me hard. "We're not leaving. Call her room and invite her down, or forget her forever. Just make a choice—I want a drink, and just because some chick turned you down in the past doesn't mean that I'm going thirsty. And you're buying."

Actually, that plan wasn't half bad, but there was one little problem. "I don't want her father to answer the phone," I began to tell Rico, but he was already walking toward the bar because he wasn't the least bit interested in this soap opera. I followed him, but I didn't call Madeline. I sat there and watched Rico have a great time with the lovelies at the bar while I wallowed in my depression. If a woman came up to talk to me, I'd get rid of her with my sullen mug. By the end of the night, I was so tired that we just ended up getting rooms at the hotel. Rico said he'd meet me for breakfast at 9 A.M.

I had a fitful night's sleep, yet I managed to oversleep. When I finally came down for breakfast, my jaw dropped—for there was Rico, sitting at a table with Madeline Love. The two of them were laughing loudly over their pancakes and having a fan-freaking-tastic time. "Great," I grumbled.

The only sensible solution seemed to be to ignore them, so I went to the buffet line to get my food. That's when I felt Paul Love hovering over my very wide shoulders. "What are you doing here?" I asked him.

"Judging the show," he said. "And by the way, Flex, my daughter isn't with her boyfriend anymore. I almost had to kill that bastard. I hated him so much that I almost shot him in my front yard. He was a real punk." Grabbing some toast, Paul smiled and said, "Just thought you might want to know."

I stood there dumbfounded, which was enough time for Paul to give me more information. "Oh, and Flex, Madeline *wanted* to come with me when she heard you were guest posing." Pause. "Now I'm going to eat my breakfast while it's still lukewarm, and that's all I have to say," he added, grinning wickedly.

Even I had to burst into a tiny smile. Yep, things were looking up indeed. However, my little glimmer of hope was gone by the time I returned to the table and saw Rico and Madeline having such a great time together. "What's up, Rico?" I asked in a tone that said this might be his last meal.

Rico took that as his cue to stand up and leave in a quick manner. Let's just say he knew I was the jealous type.

I didn't even greet Madeline. "So you like my friend," I blurted out, and I saw her forehead crease. Yes, sports fans, I was on my way to making her mad all over again.

"Flex, I don't like your friend," she said evenly. "I've been sitting here for an hour waiting for *you*. So sit down, have breakfast with me, and stop it!"

I did stop it. Over soggy hotel pancakes, we talked and talked. "You really upset me when you were so cocky and persistent last time," she said. "I knew my boyfriend was coming to visit that night, and I didn't want the two of you getting into a fistfight." She paused and then asked me pointedly, "Why do you always act so hard?"

"I'm not hard," I said, so softly that I sounded like Michael Jackson in his later years.

"Let's make one thing perfectly clear," she said. "I don't want to be your groupie." She kept going. "I want you to treat me with respect. Have you ever treated a woman with respect?" That hit home, because except for my grandmother, mother, and Levetta, I really hadn't. In a matter of minutes, Madeline had cut right to my core, and maybe it was a little too real. But that's exactly what a good relationship is—sometimes it's so real that it leaves you a little raw.

I asked Madeline if she'd sit with me in the booth where I was signing autographs that day, and she agreed. I was one happy man . . . until I looked at my watch for about the millionth time and she still hadn't appeared. Finally, I walked around and saw Madeline sitting next to Rico. I approached them to say hello, and she ignored me. *Okay, she's playing me,* I thought. The evidence was there for the taking—they were sitting there laughing and having a great old time again. Even though I blew it off and walked away, it still hurt like hell.

Madeline followed me outside, and I blurted out, "What are you doing out here? Won't Rico miss you?"

"Look, Flex," she said, "you were busy. And just because I was talking with another man doesn't mean that anything's going on. Rico told me that you were out here and I should come talk to you. Rico is your friend—and I don't like him in that way."

Finally, Madeline told me what was bothering her the most. "I've heard about you," she said. "I heard about how you treat women, and I won't be a part of those games. I want you to be straight up with me, because that's how I'll be with you."

Somehow I believed her, and it was such a relief that I dropped my guard, which wasn't easy for me because I still had no self-esteem. I did, however, have keys to a beautiful car, so I asked her to drive around town. She agreed, and I was thrilled, because I got to show off my big, shiny new convertible.

She couldn't have cared less about the car, and at that moment, neither did I. "Can I, uh, hold your hand?" I asked once we settled into those cushy leather seats.

"You don't have to ask," she said. "Just do it." So I did.

We drove around town holding hands, and just touching her skin sent bolts of energy through me. It might not sound very romantic, but I drove her to a car wash where a lot of my friends hung out. I couldn't believe that I was pulling up in this car with this girl, who by this time I was pretending was my girlfriend.

Once we got back from washing the car, I pulled over to the side of the road to show her one of my favorite scenic spots. As we gazed at the mountains in the distance, I kissed Madeline for the first time.

"You know, I came here because of you," she said. "I had to beg my father to take me. I told him that I really wanted to see you—and he even made me drive the whole way." She went on and on. "You were so rude when you saw me get out of the elevator! I spent the entire night in my room thinking about how I drove all the way to see you. And since I hate long car drives, I was *really* hating you."

I held her close and touched her silky hair.

"I told my father that I couldn't stand you and wasn't your groupie," she continued. She spoke in one long run-on sentence, as women tend to do when they're either really mad at you or dig you a lot.

"Oh, honey, I know," I said, hugging her.

It was the first time I felt like I was truly in love. And just as one important woman entered my life, another would soon leave it.

◖─◗

Later that year, I was on a posing tour in Barcelona and received a frantic call from my sister. "She's gone," Sharalene said.

Ethel Pearl Wheeler, the best singer at her church and a woman who refused to hate anybody, had passed away. It made me sad for so many reasons, but mostly because her life wasn't celebrated in the same way that mine was. Grandmommy just cleaned houses, which she did well into her 70s, and nobody gave a medal for that sort of thing. But when my siblings and I were little, the minute we'd see her bus hit the corner, we'd run as fast as we could to meet her and carry her bags. We never considered it a job—it was an honor.

Before I went to Barcelona, Grandmommy had gotten sick, and I was afraid that she might die while I was out of the country. So I went over to that cotton-candy pink house she'd lived in all my life, and I sat beside her on her creaky old bed. I took her birdlike hand into my big muscular one, but *she* was the one who gave *me* comfort the last day I saw her alive.

"Kenny, don't be sad for me," she said in a scratchy voice. "I'm not having fun being old. If I walk, I fall down. I can't take care of myself, and you know how I hate to have anyone fussing over me."

"*I* can take care of you," I whispered.

She put a bony finger to my lips. "Shhh now. When I go, it will be okay."

I couldn't stop crying. "Grandmommy," I finally said when I could speak, "I need one last favor from you." She smiled, so I continued, "When you feel like you're going, even if I'm not there, will you promise to say 'Good-bye, Kenny' for me? Will you say it out loud?'"

I saw a little tear glisten in her eye, but she wouldn't let it slip. "Yes, baby, I promise. You know how I always keep my promises."

She asked me for a picture of my son, Kennen, because she was so fond of him. "It makes me sad that I can't keep little Kennen anymore or take him on walks. I love you both so much. You better make me a promise, Kenny."

"Anything, Grandmommy," I wept.

"When I go, I want you to put a picture of you and little Kennen in my casket—although I don't want to make it look like I'm showing any favoritism. So sneak the photo in there with me for the road," she said, winking at me. I could barely see her do that because my tears were blinding me.

"Grandma, you never let us down," I told her, and she beamed. "You had no money, but you knew the most important thing was for the family to stay together. Even when there was almost no food in the fridge, you could make a fine meal if your family was around you. If somebody was in trouble, you were there. If somebody needed money, you found some. You bought everyone in this family a car on a cleaning woman's salary. There's nothing you can't do. You're a hero."

"When it came to you, my credit was ruined, and I didn't buy you a car. I'm so sorry, Kenny," Grandma lamented.

"You gave me so much more than a car," I assured her. "You gave me my life back so many times, like that night in the shower when I tried to—"

"Hush, baby," she gently interrupted.

When I was in Europe, I heard that Grandmommy was getting sicker. I begged to be let out of the tour, but the sponsors wouldn't let me go. So I called her house daily and asked my sister to hold the phone up to her ear. "I love you, Grandmommy," I told her from a million miles away. "Did you ever think your little boy would get to see the world?"

When Sharalene came back on the phone, she told me, "I don't know what you said, but Grandmommy is smiling so big."

It was unbelievable that I didn't cry during her wake. I tried to remain strong, although I couldn't go up to the coffin. I just sat in one of those hard folding chairs remembering that on our last visit, Grandmommy had told me, "Don't be sad when I go—be happy for me. I'll be in a better place, and I won't be old anymore. The next time you see me, I'll be young again. Can you even imagine that?"

At the funeral, I sat in the back row until a few friends of mine told me that I should go up there and see her one more time or I'd be sorry for the rest of my life. They almost had to pick me up by the shoulders and carry me up to my Grandmommy. Of course, the minute I saw her sleeping so peacefully, I began to weep.

Mama was there, and for once, she was the perfect mother. "Kenny, Grandmommy is okay," she told me. "I think she's smiling. You can even touch her." My mother took my hand like I was her little boy again, and put it into Grandmommy's forever-still one. Then she walked away to give me some privacy.

I reached into my pocket and pulled out the best picture I had of Kennen and me. When no one was looking, I put it in the pocket of her dress. She wouldn't have wanted anyone to think she was showing any favoritism—but for the rest of my life, she'll always be my favorite girl.

"Good-bye, Grandmommy," I whispered. I could have sworn that I heard her say, "Good-bye, baby."

Chapter 9

"You May Never Walk Again"

To cope with losing Grandmommy, I pushed myself beyond the limits of physical endurance at the gym. And even for a card-carrying pessimist like me, 1994 started off on a high note. I won first place at both the German and French Grand Prix competitions; and those 1993 first-place trophies from the Ironman Pro and the Arnold Classic looked *so* good on the kitchen counter of my $750,000 Venice beach house. God bless America, indeed! The kid who used to sleep with cockroaches suddenly found himself sleeping on 300-count Egyptian cotton sheets under a Ralph Lauren comforter.

I was hired to do my first commercial for a national soda company, and man, I was loving the taste of Squirt—not to mention all those zeroes on the paychecks that came my way because of it. This was my first big national commercial, and to say that I was psyched would have been an understatement. Life was unbelievable.

Strangely, everything had come together due to the fact that I was the number-*two* man in the bodybuilding world. Yet all the major sports magazines were predicting that 1994 was my year. "Flex

Wheeler will be number one at the Mr. Olympia competition," they announced in black and white. Mr. Olympia was the be-all, end-all title in the bodybuilding world, and each time I read that I was the guy to beat, I felt a rush through my entire system that was more satisfying than 12 cases of Squirt. There was something about the printed word—even *I* believed it.

I read all sorts of unimaginable things about myself. One magazine wrote, "Flex Wheeler has made the most profound debut in the history of bodybuilding." And then, as if my ego needed another Adrenalin shot, along came something that really blew my mind. Arnold Schwarzenegger—the Terminator himself—decided to talk about me. I figured that he sort of knew me since I'd won his Arnold Classic Bodybuilding Competition during the previous year, but this was beyond my wildest dreams. Arnold told the media that "Flex Wheeler is one of the greatest bodybuilders of all time."

Of all time (or so said Arnold).

Someone needed to lift my rather large body off the floor.

Every single time I read his words (which was about ten million times), I thought he was talking about someone else. Then I'd see *my* name attached to the beginning of that sentence, and I'd remember that it was for real. In a strange turn of events, I shocked myself by forcing down all my usual negativity, because my body wasn't just pumped—my mind was, too. I thought there was no end to what I could do. I was the man. In fact, the Squirt people were so thrilled with the commercial shoot that they asked me how soon I'd consider doing another one. I'd drive around in my Mercedes convertible—which cost $105,000, more than my father made during my entire childhood—grinning like the Cheshire cat.

One day I pulled my wheels into the gym, and that's where I ran into Dr. Dre, the internationally famous rap star. "Hey, Flex!" he called out to me. We clapped each other on the back, and Dre said, "We're so proud of you. In fact, why don't you hang with us?" I wasn't sure who "us" was, but I soon got my answer when Dre invited me to a party to celebrate the release of rapper Snoop Dogg's new CD.

Dre and the boys had rented a cruise ship, which was docked in the crystal-clear waters of the Pacific. When I pulled up in my rental car (mine was in the shop), I took off my Ray-Bans and did a double take. I couldn't believe that I was rubbing shoulders with Dre, Snoop, and their boys at a place that looked like it came out of a magazine. Could anybody stop me?

I found myself getting the kind of star treatment that's usually reserved for those who have a hit record or number-one movie. One of Dre's minions ran up to park my car, and I was immediately ushered into what looked like the coolest episode ever of *Lifestyles of the Rich and Shameless.*

Everywhere I looked were TV, movie, and music stars. Rapper Queen Latifah was there, and so was Ice Cube. Another bunch of rappers were playing pool and high-fiving each other. Strippers lounged everywhere in various states of undress, and they insisted that they'd "do anything" for you if you just asked. Meanwhile, there was smoking, drinking, eating, and much more. Frankly, I didn't participate in any of the above. I was in training, and I didn't smoke, eat much, drink, or touch any drugs—after all, the steroids were enough. And anyway, I wanted to be completely sober to soak all this in, because one day I'd tell my grandkids about it.

Glancing across the shimmering water, I could see Dre's Ferrari parked in the private lot, and a slow smile spread across my lips. I thought of how many kids from the streets dream about this type of night, and here I was living it. "Dawg," I said to Dre, who now had his arms wrapped around me like I was a long-lost relative, "when will you let me drive that Ferrari?"

"Call me, brother. You can use it anytime," he said, checking out my rented Mercedes, which was parked on the dock.

I had the time of my life that night. Yet even though everything seemed great, one part of my life wasn't going as well as it could have. I was seeing Madeline, but she was way off in San Jose, and I've gotta admit that I wasn't the most faithful boyfriend. As I stood on the boat at 2 A.M., I should have been exhausted, but I wasn't. I got the bright idea to call this girl Angie on my cell phone. "Baby, I'm coming over," I announced, hanging up on her before she could even respond. Who was going to say no to me?

After I said good-bye to Dre and Snoop, I waited about three seconds for my car, promised to hang out again with this crew, and then I hightailed it down the 10 Freeway outside the sparkling lights of Los Angeles.

I felt like I was superhuman as the rental moved along at more than 170 miles per hour. Speed was never scary to me, so I pushed the pedal down to the floor. In an instant, the little needle on the speedometer went into the red, which meant that I was going about 190. This pissed me off. The rental car was faster than my own car. "Damn it!" I cursed as if this was truly one of life's problems. A few minutes later, I muttered, "I spend fucking $105,000 on a car and . . . "

I didn't finish my thought because my eyes slowly drooped closed. When I felt my head falling forward, I shook myself awake. Training for eight hours then going to the party had suddenly caught up with me. A few minutes later, I felt my eyes close again, and I willed them to open, but they stayed shut.

The next thing I remember was a horrible *SLAM!* I woke up inside a car that was going haywire, knowing in the pit of my stomach that I'd lost control and had sent the vehicle into a spin. The sheer force of the rapid-fire circles I was spinning in jettisoned me out of the driver's seat, and then I slammed hard into the passenger seat. Somehow I could see that the speedometer was still at 140 miles per hour, although my foot wasn't on the gas.

I don't know why, but at that moment, I found myself laughing. I knew that I was one of the lucky ones, and this would be another close call. Right? Didn't these lessons always end with the person winding up drenched in sweat but much wiser? When the car stopped spinning, I'd certainly drive to my lady friend's house at a sensible speed, make love to her, and then call it a night.

But that's not what happened.

When I noticed the headlights of the oncoming cars, my adrenaline began to pound hard. A second later, the survivor part of me reasoned that I hadn't hit anything yet, which meant that just maybe I'd end up being okay. But then the road left me. At least the highway concrete I'd been careening on was gone and was replaced by some sort of rough terrain that I thought might be grass or rock. I was still spinning, but I wasn't on the freeway anymore. In that moment of pure horror, I blacked out.

Only God knows how long it was until I came to. I was on the side of an embankment—I could feel grass and rock under my fingers, which were suspiciously wet. My God, it was blood! *My* blood! I looked up and saw a light post near me. In fact, it was embedded in the front of the rental car, which was engulfed by clouds of thick white smoke. Much later, I was told by witnesses that my car actually hit the light pole, flipped off the freeway, and suddenly burst into so many sparks that it looked like a firecracker. They also saw me get out of the car and stumble around before finally passing out in the dirt and grass.

Another miraculous event happened around that time. My good buddy Rico was just getting off work, and he always took "the 10," as Angelenos call it, to get home. He actually passed what he'd later call "the worst accident I've ever seen in my life." For a year afterwards, Rico would refuse to tell me what he saw that night because it was so traumatic.

"I slowed down, and I remember thinking, *Jesus, whoever was in that car obviously didn't make it,*" Rico later said. A mile past the wreck, a sick feeling began to form in the pit of his stomach, as he realized that the car looked exactly like my rental. He quickly got on the first off-ramp and circled back around. He drove past the twisted metal the second time, which is when he saw me kneeling, almost in prayer, on the side of the road.

Rico told me that he nearly got in an accident himself when he forced his own car off the road. When he reached me, he began to cry, because, as he told me, "You looked like someone who was dead, but whose eyes were trying to hold on. It looked like you were seeing, but there was nothing there."

All I can remember is the headlights of my now-crushed rental cutting like laser beams through the steam pouring out of the engine. I remember touching my face and it was really wet, like I'd just splashed it with water at the gym. But I wasn't at the gym, and this wasn't water—it was more of my blood, and I could feel it trickling down my neck. I could see a figure coming toward me, one who looked suspiciously like my training partner.

"Rico? Is that you?" I asked. Maybe I was hallucinating. I prayed with all my might that none of this was actually happening. "What happened, man?" I asked.

"Flex, you were in an accident," Rico said, crouching next to me and grabbing my hand.

"Wow," I said. "Am I okay? Do you think I'm going to be okay?"

Rico wouldn't say anything.

"Man, what are those things hanging from my face?" I asked him, and Rico began to sob, which is something I'd never seen him do. "Is it grass and dirt? Can you please help me wipe it off?"

He didn't lift a finger; instead, he just cried harder. Later, I found out that I'd been bleeding for so long that the blood had dried like icicles, and these "bloodcicles" were suspended from my face, hanging on by their own thready fibers. Rico also saw that clumps of tissue and skin were hanging off my face, stuck on in the wrong spots by sweat and dried blood.

It seemed like it took forever, but an ambulance finally did arrive. The paramedics told me to keep still as they cut my pants off my body.

"Don't cut my pants—they're so nice and expensive," I begged them. Then something really bad occurred to me: Was there something wrong with my legs? I couldn't really feel them anymore.

"Sir, we need to cut them off. You were in an accident," said one baby-faced EMT.

"I was in a . . . what?" I stammered. *"No! I can't be in an accident! I'm supposed to win Olympia this year!"* I kept screaming, "NO, NO, NO!"

The EMT turned to Rico and asked him, "Do you think he had anything to drink tonight?"

"No way, man," Rico said. "I'm his training partner, and he's a champion athlete. He doesn't drink."

"Do you think he did any drugs?" the EMT quizzed Rico.

"I told you no!" Rico yelled. "Stop asking me these questions! It's an insult to be saying this stuff!"

On the word *stuff,* I blacked out again. The next thing I remember was a big blinding-white light. For a minute, I thought that maybe I got to heaven, but no. It was Cedars-Sinai Hospital, and I was in the emergency room and in the most severe pain of my life. When I could collect my thoughts, I noticed that I wasn't in a bed, which seemed strange. Instead, I was attached to a straight board with my head held in place by thick pieces of adhesive tape that didn't allow me to move an inch.

"Don't even try to move, Mr. Wheeler," a nurse implored.

For some reason, I thought of Hedy, the woman I'd been dating before I met Madeline. I began to scream, "Get Hedy! Get Hedy!" It turns out that as I was doing this, Hedy was actually at the front desk filling out paperwork. At the time, I didn't have any health insurance, and the hospital wasn't sure if they were going to continue to help me. Unbelievably, Hedy gave them her American Express card and said, "Just charge whatever he needs. Anything." My being able to walk today, and the medical care I received that night are because of her generosity, which proves that even at the worst moments in life, you can often find the best in people.

At that moment, however, I couldn't worry about money or insurance or paying an ex-girlfriend back for her kindness. Doctors were entering the room with what looked like long tweezers, and my stomach lurched because I just knew that this was going to be painful. Dipping the tweezers into alcohol, the head doc gave the instructions to begin. For the next hour, the team pulled shards of glass out of my face, one by one. Some of it was embedded so deeply in my cheeks that my screams turned into actual howls that would rival any wolf in the wild. They couldn't deaden my pain with drugs, because I had to tell them where to locate the glass. In other words, one doctor would rub his hand across my face until my eyes filled with tears and I moaned in pain. Then they'd dig until they found that piece of glass in my face. Some of the pieces were really large, and the docs pulled them out bit by agonizing bit, which felt like pure torture.

Every few minutes a nurse would pour peroxide over my entire head to get rid of the dried blood, and then we'd begin again. They pulled pieces of glass out of my ears and out of my forehead as well. Finally, I was completely exhausted. "Just leave the rest in me," I pleaded, but the main doctor just shook his head.

"We have a long way to go tonight, Flex," he said. "After this, we have to stitch your ear back on. It was almost completely ripped off."

For a minute, they allowed Rico; my manager, Robin Chang; and my friends Paul and Chris into the room with me. Paul saw me first and burst into tears. Soon the other guys were sobbing, too, and then they did something strange for tough guys—they stood there holding hands like they were in a group prayer session. *God, I must look awful,* I thought.

After the glass was out and my ear was on, they kept me on that hard board. I was informed that I still wasn't supposed to move my head. "But I hurt," I sobbed.

"I know," a nurse told me. "There's still a lot of glass embedded in your back, but we can't move you."

Next, the doctors put me and the board into an MRI machine, because they needed to see how I was doing internally. I felt extremely claustrophobic, but the docs insisted that they had to see what was going on in my back. "What's the matter with me?" I asked, and then it hit me—I was on that board for a reason.

I was paralyzed.

Sure enough, the diagnosis was that I'd broken the C5 and C6 bones in my spine, plus I had a fracture running through my collarbone and right shoulder.

So *this* was going to be my story? I'd come a hair away from being a world-class champion athlete, only to drive home a little too fast and wind up paralyzed? It was so unfair and so unreal that I felt like I was the butt of one very cruel joke. But some real comedy did get thrown in the mix—Rico, Paul, and Chris were trying anything to amuse me, including pretending to steal hospital supplies like bandages and syringes. This happened during the five minutes every hour they were allowed to duck their heads in and see me. Even in my pain, I felt my lips try to curl into a smile. God, I loved those guys.

The nightmare continued the next day when the doc sat down on my bedside as if he were too upset to stand. "Flex, first of all, I have to be honest with you. We're not sure if you'll ever walk again," he said.

Boom! There it was—right in my face.

Of course, I couldn't live with that diagnosis for one simple reason. "Doc, I have Olympia in a few months. October 17 to be exact," I told him in a very businesslike tone. "I have to walk because I have to run. That's how I get ready for Olympia. I run three hours a day on a treadmill because I'm an athlete. So think of something . . . and fast."

The doctor's eyes welled up with tears. "Son, you're not going to make it," he said.

Wait, now I was going to die? "No," said the kindly old doc. "You're not going to make Olympia this year. Maybe not *any* year. I'm really sorry." He began to explain exactly what was wrong with me, but it was like I was underwater, and he was yelling these things from the surface. It came out as one big blob of words that made no sense.

A few seconds later, my own tears began to flow. "My whole life is over," I kept repeating. Then I began to scream: "My life is over! I want to die! I want to die!" The doc called for a sedative, and the world went fuzzy for a few hours.

What followed were some of the most degrading moments of my entire life. No one had bothered to wash me since the accident, and I began to stink to the point that I called the head nurse in and begged her to help me. I was still attached to the board, and I couldn't move a muscle. This wonderful lady, a large woman with big hands, gently used sponges to get the dried blood off of me. I still had glass embedded in my back, so she had to be really careful. Again, I was blown away by the concern and kindness of a total stranger.

The nurse went out of the room for a few minutes to talk to the doctor, who agreed that the damage was done and I didn't need to be on the board anymore. Slowly, they lowered me into a wheelchair, and I waited for a miracle to happen like in the movies. But there wouldn't be one today, as I still couldn't feel the lower half of my body.

The nurse stripped me naked, and I could see dried blood caked all over me. She had an idea to wheel me into the shower room.

"Okay, I'll take it from here," I whispered when she turned the water on.

"Honey, I have to stay with you," she said.

"But I want to clean myself," I begged, asking for just a little dignity.

"No, I'm sorry. *I* have to clean you. You can hurt yourself if you move the wrong way—hurt yourself even worse," she said, telling it to me straight.

I was absolutely powerless. I was one of the strongest men in the country, but I couldn't even find the strength to grasp a bar of soap and wash my own face. Here I was, a fully grown man, and this woman had to clean me. I felt so awful and pathetic that I began to weep huge tears.

The nurse was really angry by now, but not at me. "I can't believe they haven't cleaned you. You are really ripe!" she said, reminding me of my grandmother. She got the job done, cleaning me of the dirt, blood, sweat, and urine that had clung to me. I was so grateful to wash away some of that accident.

That night in bed and off the board, I began having nightmares that someone was trying to kill me. I guess they had me on some extreme meds that were causing me to hallucinate, because I saw someone enter my hospital room with hands like an ape, and suddenly they were trying to choke the life from me. The harder I tried to rip these demon hands from my neck, the more pain I felt.

Hedy, my ex, was staying in my room, and she woke me up because my hands were on my neck brace. I was trying to rip the thing off me, which could have caused even worse damage to my spine.

Five days later, I improved a bit. I had enough control to sit up in bed (in a complete head-to-toe metal body brace), which doctors proclaimed "a true miracle." I was in blinding, white-hot, shattering pain while I sat there, but I refused to lie down again. I wasn't going down again. Ever. I'd sit up for the rest of my life if that's what it took. Every once in a while, I'd let out a high-pitched scream because it hurt so bad. I still refused to lie down. I convinced myself that this was just another day of training, another day of pushing my body.

A few days later, Dr. Dre came to see me, and the minute I looked into his eyes, I started to cry. Later on, I found out that he hardly ever went to the hospital because he couldn't stand to see anyone sick, so it meant a lot for him to come.

Another day, athlete and actor Lou Ferrigno, who had played The Hulk on TV, walked through my door. He carried a killer box of chocolates, which he had to put down on my feeding table when he saw my face and twisted-up body. He couldn't keep his hands from shaking, and holding that box made it even more obvious. "Oh, you'll be okay, Flex," he announced, trying to sound cheerful. But his eyes betrayed him with the type of look you give someone a few minutes before they croak.

My auto insurance company thought that I *had* died in the crash. "We're assuming this was a fatal accident?" said the man on the other end of the phone. He was shocked when I told him that I wasn't speaking from the grave—I'd actually lived after tumbling around in a car that wasn't only crushed, but in their terms "double totaled."

Plain and simple, I was a mess, and the last thing I needed was to have my family getting upset, so I called my sister with one big request. "Don't come see me," I insisted. "Don't tell Daddy or Mama." Of course, Sharalene did show up, and the look on her face broke my heart. When she thought I was sleeping, she called my father, and I'll never forget her words: "Just be ready."

The day my friend Ty Maguire showed up, it was almost surreal. He walked up to my bed, turned on his heel, and walked out the door as if he couldn't take it. When he came back in, he never once looked at me—he'd pin his eyes to the ground, the ceiling, or the window . . . anything but me. He kept repeating the same thing: "You're going to be okay, man. You're going to be okay."

"But what do I look like?" I finally asked, afraid of the answer. I'd been begging a nurse to give me a hand mirror, and she kept saying that she wasn't allowed to do so because it might prove to be "too upsetting." On this day, she finally gave in. Handing me her own compact, she looked down the entire time, and bolted from the room after I took the little reflective surface into my swollen hands. I said a silent prayer to God, and then I moved the mirror into position and tried to focus on what was left of my image.

Chunks of my hair were missing, and a lot of the skin was ripped off my face. I moved the gauze away to see what had been left. My face was mostly huge, gooey patches of torn muscle and yellow tissue lying there like chicken fat you skim off soup. There were stitches everywhere, making me look like Frankenstein's younger brother. I couldn't even stare into the same eyes that had looked back at me for my entire life, because thanks to my head trauma, blood vessels had burst all over the place, including inside my eyes. One of my eyes was so red inside that I couldn't even make out my own pupil.

"Nurse!" I bellowed, handing the scared young lady her mirror back. By now, both of us were bawling.

This was seven days into my hospital stay, so I could only imagine how bad I'd looked when I had been wheeled in the night of the accident. I began to get terrible panic attacks, telling the nurses that I didn't think I could breathe. On the way home from the hospital a few days later—yes, there was nothing more they could do so they released me—I had another panic attack and just *knew* I was suffocating.

I was certain that they shouldn't release me, and I was partially right, because it got so bad with the panic attacks that the hospital had to hook up an oxygen tank in my house. Meanwhile, I couldn't do anything for myself. I was in a wheelchair, with instructions to move as little as possible so my spine could heal. I couldn't even go to the bathroom by myself, and I needed help adjusting my neck brace. The one bit of good news I heard before I left the hospital was that I might walk again—but there were no promises.

Interestingly enough, I was told that my training as a bodybuilder had saved my mobility, if not my life. "The only thing that saved your spine from cracking in two was the tremendous amount of muscles that you've built around your spinal cord," said one doc. "In fact, your thick muscles are what saved your spinal cord from being severed in half during the accident."

I didn't consider myself a religious man at that point in my life (that would come later), yet somehow I knew that it wasn't really my muscles that saved me—it was God himself.

At least I was never alone, because my ex-girlfriends took shifts camping out on my couch, which made them true angels of mercy. But in the dead of night while they were asleep, I'd replay the accident in my mind. The police told me that as I'd fallen asleep at the wheel, the car had begun to drift to the side of the road. The car ramming against the embankment had woken me up, and I'd reflexively yanked the wheel the other way, which caused me to go into a spin. That's when the right tire blew, which made the car spin even faster.

The cops also told me that my car actually drove partially up a light pole, flipped up in the air, and then landed with a thud back on the freeway. The doctors said that at that point my brain had shut off, as if someone had flicked a switch. It was my own internal safety mechanism—thank God our bodies actually protect themselves from the shock and horror of traumatic experiences. My brain might have checked out, but my memories of the accident still floated back at me in full Technicolor.

That's how come I know I died. I remember talking to Rico at the accident site, yet it was as if I were hovering above both of us, gazing in awe at him and my crumpled body down below. I was a few feet above him, and in no pain at that point. I was also well above myself when they wheeled me into the hospital. I escaped my own body again in the operating room, only to think it strange that so many people were racing around me when I felt better than I had in my entire life. In fact, I felt euphoric. I guess these were *out-of-body experiences*. Each time it was like I was right above the heads of those surrounding me, like I had really cool ringside seats to the main event.

I only wished for that gentle time again as I dealt with the day-to-day grind of putting my broken body back together. The good news was that it was becoming clearer that I *would* walk again. The results didn't come from weeks of rehab work at some hospital, though. One day in the privacy of my own bedroom, I got myself up with some help from one of the girls, and I took a few steps toward the bathroom. The pain was searing, but those few steps led to walking across the room. Eventually I progressed to a walker and then a cane. My first step without any assistance made me want to drop to my knees and say a prayer of thanks.

Unfortunately, I'd soon find out that the hurtful elements in my life wouldn't be limited to physical distress. The first bit of bad news came my way before my butt was even home from the hospital. It turns out that my sponsor, Joe Weider, and his sports company—the one that was paying me a monthly salary—heard about my accident and immediately fired me. They didn't even wait for the blood to be washed away. They just sent a letter by registered mail, and it basically said that I'd broken my agreement with them because I'd promised to compete in bodybuilding shows, and now I obviously couldn't do that anymore. In other words, I was history. That letter was the only correspondence I ever received from them.

I tried to call Joe to state my case. Lying down to my core, I told his secretary that the doc said I'd be A-OK, and I'd be competing, no, make that *winning,* in a few weeks. But he never returned my calls, which was just as shocking as the company never bothering to call or send flowers when I was in the hospital. I was clearly *over* in their eyes.

When I got home, they sent a fax reminding me of current events. It said: "Mr. Wheeler, your contract has been terminated. Good luck in the future."

Future? I didn't have one of those.

Chapter 10

Trying to End It All

I was sprung from the hospital in early June 1994 and was put into bed to vegetate until mid-September. I was 29 years old—a prisoner of my own circumstances and the carnage that was my body. I couldn't find any relief anywhere, so I started to think about finishing what the accident had started. I wanted to just end it, once and for all.

Pity was my old friend, and now we were hanging out together on a minute-by-minute basis. The only other emotion I let register was fury. I'd been at a point in my life where no one could stop me, and lo and behold, I'd stopped myself. The questions hit me like bricks: Why did I go to that stupid party? Why was I driving so fast? How could I have fallen asleep at the wheel?

Pain and depression made one hell of a dangerous cocktail. Each day I woke up crying, and I didn't turn off the waterworks until late at night. In the hallway, I could hear my ex-girlfriends whispering that they didn't know what to do with me. I heard the words "suicide watch," and I guess that's what they had me under. Little did they know that I wasn't just *thinking* about ending my life—I attempted it quite a few times when their prying eyes weren't looking.

When I was alone, I'd twirl around the handgun that I'd secretly kept from my days on the police force. I'd sit slumped on the edge of my mattress and think about where I'd put the bullet—my head, my gut, my big old chest? I'd weigh the pros and cons of each spot: The head was too messy; if I aimed for the gut, I might miss a vital organ and live; and the chest seemed tricky because I didn't exactly know how to find the center of my heart. I was very coldhearted about the whole thing, and even scheduled time for target practice. When I'd hear that day's jailer leave to go to the store, I'd get out the gun, aim at whatever was handy in my bedroom, and pull the trigger. My good gold dress watch? *Boom!* It was shot to smithereens. The leg of my nightstand? *Boom!* I was careful to only inflict surface wounds that no one could see. No need for my collective ex-girlfriends to lose it over a bunch of shot-up furniture—that could only lead to a whole bunch of questions I preferred to avoid.

As for the noise, I was surprised that none of the neighbors called the cops, but that's life in Los Angeles—a few gunshots in the distance seemed like normal, everyday background music. Yet I couldn't have cared less if an entire SWAT team surrounded my bed. I'd get into fights with my girlfriends, telling them, "I hate my life, and if you don't get out of here, I'll shoot myself dead." They'd look at me with concern and beg me to stop . . . but I couldn't.

It was even worse for my friends. I'd ask them, "Do you have a gun? You do? Maybe someday I'll force you to come over and shoot me." They'd walk out of my house baffled, and some told my girl-friends, "Flex has gone crazy. He needs to go to a shrink."

In one lucid moment, I thought that maybe what worked for other people could also help me, so I *did* go see a shrink. He asked me a few questions about my accident, gasped when he saw the gashes on my head, and diagnosed me as "depressed." Wow! Was he sure? My mechanic could have come up with the same conclusion.

This guy actually made me feel worse when I trusted him with the two most hurtful parts of my life—missing my kids, Kennen and Brandy (who didn't even know about the accident), and my childhood. He told me I could fix the first one by picking up the phone. As for the second, deep inside I knew that my pain had started with having been sexually abused as a kid. I'd always heard that if you just "talked it out," then maybe the pain would stop. Isn't that what they tell you to do?

So with all the strength I could muster, I told the shrink about my father's girlfriend, Crystal, and my relatives and how they'd made me "do it." I cried as I told him that I'd known it was wrong, but I hadn't known how to stop it.

When I was finished, he looked up from his notebook, shrugged, and said, "Flex, you need to forget about being raped. Just put it out of your mind. Our time is up."

Whoa! Wait a minute! This was worth $200 an hour? Excuse me if I got it wrong, but basically he was saying that I should push it all down even further?

"You're fine," he said as he escorted me to the door. "So you had a bad accident and a rough childhood—you just need to put it all behind you and choose to live."

What the hell? Now I know that certain shrinks really do help people, but the one I chose was an idiot. You don't take a suicidal, dangerous man and tell him to buck up and smile. When I went home, I *did* smile . . . while I held my gun.

I contemplated easier ways to kill myself, like pills and booze. The problem there was that I hate the taste of alcohol. I don't even like beer, which has always made me slightly nauseated. Still, I went out and bought a six-pack . . . which I ended up using as target practice. Yes, it was messy and smelly, but it was rather satisfying to play Clint Eastwood in the privacy of my own bedroom.

My heart ached for something or someone who could lift me from all this insanity. And then one night, I saw her face in my dreams. "You're really cocky," she said, and I touched her long, silky hair. She had the face of an angel and the backbone of ten men.

"Madeline," I said out loud, waking myself up.

I couldn't exactly remember a Madeline in my life. You see, I'd experienced memory loss during the accident, and I honestly couldn't put all the pieces together when it came to the last few years of my life. The doctors diagnosed it as both long- and short-term memory loss, and they informed me that I might never get those memories back. But a couple of weeks after I could walk again, images of this beautiful woman began to pop into my mind. By then, my ex-girlfriend

Hedy had moved in temporarily to take care of me, yet I knew she wasn't the one I was seeing in my dreams.

I began to think that I'd made up the vision of this beautiful Madeline . . . until one day the fog lifted, and I nearly doubled over in fresh pain. Slowly, it came back to me—the Marriott, Rico, the car wash, the kiss. Later, I found out that while I'd been in the hospital, Madeline had called my house a few times, but no one bothered to tell her about my accident. When I didn't call her back, she just assumed that I'd dumped her.

I didn't know any of this. All I knew is that I wanted to reach out to her, but I couldn't remember her phone number. (Before the accident, I always memorized things and never wrote them down.) I forced myself to recall it, and each number started coming to me slowly. I tried various combinations of phone numbers that were all wrong— and then it was like I'd won the lottery when she answered.

Madeline was really pissed, and my hands were shaking as I tried to tell her what had happened to me. To my surprise, another pro bodybuilder (and one of my so-called friends), had told her that I had indeed dropped her. He said that I'd given him her phone number because I was "passing her on." He even offered to fly her to Paris for a romantic weekend. Of course, she'd told him to get lost.

"You broke my heart," she told me.

"No, I broke my neck," I said.

I went on to tell her the details of my accident, and she was silent. I thought she didn't believe me, so, in frustration and despair, I hung up. I later found out that she was shocked and horrified that I'd had to go through all of this turmoil alone, and she even called her father and yelled at him for not telling her that I was in the hospital. He explained that he'd had no idea.

The next morning, Madeline called me to say that she was really sorry, and she wanted to come to me immediately. Even though I had Hedy living with me, I knew what I had to do. I stumbled downstairs and told her that I thought it would be best for us both if she moved out. I said that I'd always respect and love her for helping during my accident, but I didn't want to mess up her future. In her heart, she knew I was right, so she packed her bags.

It was a turning point for me. I knew that I was in love with Madeline, but if I wanted her, I had to get my act together. I also knew that my body was feeling stronger every day. I figured that I needed two goals to get me back on track: I'd try to attend the North America Bodybuilding Championship in New Mexico just to show everybody that I wasn't dead, and I'd make Madeline proud of me, no matter what.

I also wanted the woman I loved to be with me during what would be the hardest training period of my life, although I was mortified about what she might think when she saw me for the first time.

"Honey, I look real bad," I told her over the phone. "My head is cut up so bad that chunks of my hair are missing, and I still have a neck brace on."

"Flex, you should know by now that I don't care about any of that—I just want to see you. I wish I had wings so I could fly to you right now," she said.

When I met Madeline at the airport, she ran off the plane and into my arms. She just held me for what seemed like an eternity. She wasn't repulsed by what she saw—instead, she took my bruised hand and we boarded another plane for New Mexico.

I wore a skullcap on the entire trip, but once we got to our hotel room I knew the waiting game was over. I took off the cap, and Madeline gazed at my wrecked head with such gentle concern that my knees almost buckled. "It's not so bad," she finally said, and ordered some enchiladas from room service. This proved to me that sometimes our biggest and most paralyzing fears are just pointless wastes of energy.

We sat and talked for hours about the accident, and how the doctors had been forced to pick all of that glass out of my head and from my ears. "Thank God I never scar," I joked. (Actually, I was telling the truth—today the scars are so faint that no one would ever guess that I'd been in an accident.) I also told Madeline about how I'd been thinking about killing myself. "I can't promise you that this won't happen again," I warned.

She didn't really understand, but she still wanted to stick by me and try to help me heal. She wanted to move in with me, and the idea filled me with joy and dread, because I knew that my emotions were still as unpredictable as a summer storm.

After we returned to Los Angeles, the storm warnings were everywhere. Maybe it was seeing all those bodybuilders onstage looking like they didn't have a care in the world. I talked to Rico and Robin about it, and they both told me that if I wanted to come back, it would be a tough climb. "It won't be impossible, but we'll have our backs against the wall. I'm game if you are, but it's your call, Flex," Robin said.

And Rico added, "But you just need to know that it might never happen for you again. You have to wrap your mind around the idea that it could be over."

That left me depressed and suicidal once more, so I started to sit in bed and play with the stupid gun again.

Madeline would walk in and say, "Give me the damn gun, Flex."

Instead, I'd point it at the wall near her. At least I had the presence of mind not to point the gun *at* her. Now the first lesson when it comes to guns is that you should always respect them and treat them as if they might go off at any second. That's why you never, ever point a gun at someone unless you mean it. The scary part is that at times, I *did* mean it. When my mind went wild, I thought about killing both Madeline and myself, but deep down I was a total coward. I couldn't kill myself, and I knew that I could never hurt her in a million years.

Madeline wasn't afraid, even when I started to demolish her things. I saw her gym shoes on the floor and shot them. *Kaboom!* They were gone. Her purse was in pieces. Her charm bracelet? One shot and it was gold dust. She'd simply sit down and calmly repeat, "Stop. Don't do this."

"Then I'm going to kill myself!" I'd scream.

But just because she was a petite woman doesn't mean that Madeline wasn't strong. Other girlfriends would have run out the door and never looked back. "Calm down, Flex," she'd say, stroking my unarmed hand. Then she'd present me with her open palm, and I'd place the gun inside.

"Oh my God, please don't ever tell your father about this," I begged her, as tears coursed down my face. She never did—in fact, this book will be the first time that Paul Love ever learns about how horrible I was to his daughter in the early days. If anyone ever treated *my* daughter that way, I assure you it wouldn't be pretty.

My mood swings continued. I could be romantic one night, violent the next, and depressed the night after that. I couldn't understand why Madeline would want to be with me. I was ugly and deformed—could she have wanted me for my money? But what money?

She told me that she was thinking about getting a job, but I wouldn't let her because I needed to control her. We got into some supersonic fights, and she'd pack up to leave, saying that I'd used my last chance with her. Since I shot up her suitcase during one of my rages, she had to be creative with her threats of moving out. One time she packed her clothes in paper grocery bags, called a taxi, and then went to the airport. The next morning, she was back with no explanation other than "I love you. Why? I don't know."

One night when I was acting more rational than usual, she said, "Flex, you need help. You need real counseling. You've got some serious issues."

"I think it has to do with my past," I told her quietly. "I think those early rapes are why I don't care about myself or respect myself. I don't care if I live or die, because a lot of folks didn't when I was a kid."

I told Madeline the painful details of my abuse, and I shared the shame I felt with her. But she didn't pass any judgments. She just listened, held me when my body crumpled into a wasteland of pain, and helped me see that I was the only one in the situation who *shouldn't* be ashamed. I was the victim.

I continued to be honest with her—I told her about how I'd slept with many, many women in all states and countries when I was on the road at bodybuilding competitions. "I'd meet a girl in a club, and by the time we got to first names, everything resembling clothing was off," I explained. "I'm not looking for an easy out, but maybe my being very promiscuous has to do with what happened to me sexually as a kid," I said. "I was so used to females being attracted by my money or fame that I couldn't even recognize a great woman until I met you."

I even confessed to Madeline that I'd cheated on her during those early months when we were first dating, and amazingly enough, she didn't hate me for what I'd done. She even did something that few would have expected—she forgave me.

Other people had a lot to say about her reaction. "She's playing you," my brother Darnell told me, adding. "A woman that beautiful is not going to put up with your crap." Even my sister said, "I think she's just after your money. This is a woman who has probably had so many guys running a game on her that she's not good for anyone anymore."

I was so in love with Madeline by now that she had the power to really rip my heart out. As each day passed, however, I noticed that my heart was still right there in place. This woman wasn't around to take anything . . . she just wanted to give.

⊙—⊙

Rico wanted me to give bodybuilding another shot.

"Dawg, are you insane?" I finally asked him.

He laughed. "Yeah, I'm insane, but not as nuts as you. I'll meet you at the gym tomorrow morning at nine. Oh, and leave the gun at home."

That was it. One day in late September 1994, I woke at dawn and dug out my old workout clothes. I laced up my training shoes and walked out the door on my own two feet. I felt the power in each step.

The minute I burst into the gym, Rico eyed me and treated me just like the old days. "Well, are you going to stand there or hit the weight bench?" he demanded.

Sitting on that cold leather bench, I experienced a feeling that was new to me in a gym—I was scared. It wasn't adrenaline pumping through my system, but self-doubt. "Too much time has passed," I finally said as I struggled with weights I could have easily lifted in the old days. Since the accident, I'd pretty much lost everything I had in terms of muscle mass.

"Let's start with 20 light reps," Rico said, ignoring me.

"Do you honestly think that I'll be able to compete at my old level?" I asked, grunting as I slowly and painfully lifted the bar.

"I didn't honestly think you'd show up today," he replied. "What happens from this point on is anyone's guess, Dawg."

In October, I attended Olympia 1994 as a paying spectator. Robin was on one side of me and Madeline was on the other, but their support just wasn't enough. Almost from the minute the show began,

I was crying because I wanted to be up there so badly. Bottom line—I just wasn't ready.

However, the doctors had completely released me. They told me that it was okay to work out *moderately,* cheerfully telling me that I could do some light walking. But by that time, I was already beyond moderate at the gym. I was running two miles a day on my treadmill, and I was also squatting 315 pounds—the weights were being lifted by those savior muscles in my back, the stretchy supports that cushioned my spinal cord from snapping in half during my accident.

I know it sounds like I was doing well, but I was so out of sync that I could barely get a few reps in. I was trying to take my brain out of my injury, and I just couldn't wipe away the horror of what had happened to me. Instead of seeing my body as being strong, I saw it as broken. Plus, I was really embarrassed to step into Gold's Gym every morning because I'd lost so much weight. Feeling inadequate and weak, I'd tell Rico, "I don't belong here. I'm a scrawny chicken."

Robin would wander in and say, "Yes, you do belong. Let's try another set. Get your ass in gear."

But I'd watch the other bodybuilders keep track of the little amount of weight the late, great Flex Wheeler was using, and I'd feel like a failure.

Charles Glass, my old trainer, stopped by and told me, "In six months, they'll envy the weight you have up there. Keep going."

I went back on the steroids. By the end of the year, I was back to squatting 595 pounds, and it wasn't killing me like when I first did the measly 315. I repeated to myself, "Okay, you've been injured and you broke your neck. Let that hurt person go now and get back in the groove."

I thought about entering the Arnold Classic in February even though I had no time to get back into contest shape. I was really forcing the issue—I shouldn't have even been thinking about competing this quickly after breaking my neck, fracturing my right collarbone, and trying to heal up numerous facial lacerations that had caused my eyes to swell shut and turn blood red. It was the height of insanity.

Luckily I wasn't a *lonely* lunatic. Madeline would stop by the gym and help me work out by just being incredibly supportive. I leaned on her in the most important ways. On the outside, I started to look like I was made out of stone again, but inside I was still as soft as a feather pillow. I can honestly say that it wasn't the bed rest or the working out that healed me—Madeline put me back together in every way possible and made me the man I am today. Her medicine was encouragement. Her therapy was love. Her bandage was standing her own ground and not taking any of my crap. She didn't allow me to be a child who could just lash out and scream or grab a gun. Because of her strength, she forced me to grow into a man.

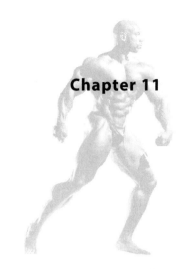

Chapter 11

"He's Back"

Charles, Rico, and Robin were also integral parts of my healing. "You can do it," Rico told me so many times that his lips almost fell off.

"It's just a matter of time," Robin would chime in.

I had tremendous support, even on the days when I felt so stiff and sore that I couldn't move. At first I had so little neck movement that I couldn't turn fully to the left or the right, and I wondered if I'd ever have that flexibility in my neck again.

What made it worse were the tension headaches I got after working out. The throbbing pain stayed in my head, sometimes for days—at times I felt like my brain would burst. My spirit, however, wouldn't crumble.

I started off 1995 by doing a few shows just to get back in the swing of things. I started with the Florida Invitational Bodybuilding Show. I guess my accident hadn't made the news in the Sunshine State, but by the time I got there, word had spread. Man, the first time I walked backstage, I could feel eyes drilling into me, as if people were expecting some kind of freak show. I was also sent a message from one of the other athletes: "We heard about your neck, but we're not going to take it easy on you because you got hurt."

"I don't need any favors," I replied, and my detractor immediately shut up.

When I walked onstage during that competition, there was a warm round of applause and cheers from the crowd, but I told myself that it didn't mean anything unless I won first place.

A few hours later, I heard a few words that humbled me: "The winner is Flex Wheeler!"

Thank You, God, I thought. This was about as far away from "You may never walk again" as I could get.

I was out of my mind with happiness. My big reward for winning a show was always a Domino's pan pizza, and Madeline had one waiting for me backstage. But I told her, "Today I want the Domino's *and* a cinnamon-and-cheese Danish." The smell was killing the other guys, who were now seriously ticked off because I had the prize *and* the all the good snack food. "Do we have some Nacho Cheese Doritos, too?" I asked Madeline before giving her a big gooey cinnamon kiss.

When I got home, it was rough to stay in that excited mode. Yes, I was making a comeback, but I still didn't feel 100 percent. I wasn't eating properly—instead I existed on liquid protein, carb drinks, and steroids. That's a really dangerous way to live; plus, I didn't feel strong because my insulin levels were all over the map. I knew that I needed to make some changes, so I saw a nutritionist who put me on a sensible plan that combined carbs and lean proteins.

Later that February, I competed in the Ironman Pro. "Flex Wheeler is back," the announcer said, and the crowd roared their approval. Before the accident, I was 227 pounds. I lost 20 pounds during my time off, and that loss was all muscle. I came to the 1995 Ironman Pro even skinnier at 216 and really flat, which is a bodybuilding term—but not a good one. Bodybuilders want bulk to come in the form of *muscle,* not pounds.

Besides my own personal issues with my body, I once again noticed that the other bodybuilders weren't exactly thrilled that I was back. Of course they didn't want to see me hurt, but they didn't want me interfering with their income either.

"Oh, great, he's back," griped one of the builders backstage, as if I couldn't hear him.

When I walked onstage, I told myself, *You're starting over from scratch*. I felt like an amateur out there until I saw Madeline, Robin, and Rico—my posse—in the audience. I kept my eyes on them the entire time, and they didn't stop smiling and instructing me.

You see, over the years my boys and I came up with a whole signal system that the military might find impressive. For instance, if they held up one finger, it meant I was number one out there. Rico would point to his shoes if I was doing well, which meant, "Flex, you have big boots on," or I was kicking everyone's butt. During intermission, if I was doing really well, they'd yell, "It's the Flex Wheeler Show!" If I was doing only so-so, they'd hold up their fists to let me know I had to fight.

Let's just say that at the Ironman, it *was* "The Flex Wheeler Show." I came in first place, even though no one could believe it. I guess I had some big boots on indeed. It was a great victory for me for obvious reasons, but mostly, it was a slap in the face to everyone who thought that Flex Wheeler was dead and buried. I had risen from the ashes.

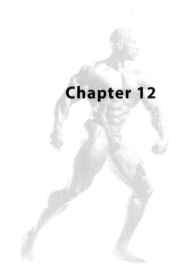

Chapter 12

A Life-Sized Action Hero

After my win at the 1995 Ironman, I was ready to jump back in to competitive bodybuilding full time. I went on to grab a second-place trophy at the Arnold Classic, which wasn't bad considering my circumstances—but when I came in eighth at Olympia, I was a sad camper indeed.

I decided to sweat through my pain, but my showing at Olympia was a wake-up call. *You aren't where you need to be,* I told myself. *Your legs are jelly and your arms are noodles.* Of course, this wasn't even close to the truth, but I still liked to beat up on myself. That negative voice continued on. *You barely won those last two trophies. You're a bullshit artist, a loser, a . . .* well, you get the idea.

I'd wake up to do my cardio routine, and those dark thoughts were my mental workout. In a weird way, these doubts helped a bit because they kept me from getting too comfortable, and reminded me that I had a long road ahead. It would take me the better part of a year to build myself back up, but I was on my way. Before I knew it, I was gripping a first-place statue at the South Beach Pro in 1996. For a few minutes, I gave myself a break—I felt the joy, and it was great.

Looking at the pile of bills with "late" stamped on them was just damn annoying. I was still living on a portion of my former income, and the sad truth was that I could no longer afford my mortgage payments. Banks don't care if you're a *former* sports champion, so I had no choice but to regroup and sell my dream house on the beach. Good-bye, Mercedes. So long, gold jewelry. As each of my possessions faded away, I found that I didn't really miss *them,* I missed the idea of what they stood for in my life—success. I was no longer a winner in my mind, and that stung.

But even during the bleakest of times, I've always been blessed by people who have stepped up to help me. An old friend named Neil allowed Madeline and me to move into an "extra" condo he just happened to own, and we ended up staying there for a year. It was a godsend, because I honestly don't know where we would have gone if not for his generosity.

Meanwhile, I kept waiting for one of those checks with all the zeroes on the end to arrive. But my endorsement deals weren't back in place, and Joe Weider wasn't exactly my fairy godfather, although he did reinstate my contract—after cutting it to a third of what it was before my accident. He eventually ended up bringing it back up to half of what I was making, and promised to up it considerably if I continued to prove myself. I did just that—I won the Ironman Pro in 1996 and came in first at the Night of Champions that same year. Finally, Weider reinstated my old contract, but he told me that the company had been disappointed with my performance at Olympia that year (I came in fourth). "It's beneath you, Flex," he said, shaking his head with disdain.

Weider was a man of few words, but each one was like a shot in the gut. Of course, someone thinking the worst of me was all it took to jettison me into despair, but part of me was also seriously angry. I'd nearly died the year before, and the mere fact that I was able to walk on a stage at all was a pretty big deal. I'm not exactly sure why nobody in that company said, "We're amazed at your progress, Flex. Way to go!"—especially when you consider that Weider had other athletes who were perfectly healthy and under contract but couldn't even qualify for Olympia. I was the guy recovering from a broken neck, and now I was the fourth-best bodybuilder in the world. But I guess it still wasn't number one.

"You'll be back even better than before," Robin promised me.

His words came true in 1997, and once I was back, baby, I was *back*. Ironman—number one, thank you very much. Arnold Classic— numero uno. San Jose Pro—whaddaya know? The sports mags called those wins my "triple crown victories." They also dubbed me "The Sultan of Symmetry."

I was 31 years old, 300 pounds, and 5'10" tall. My biceps measured 22¾", my chest measurements hovered around 50", my calves were 22" around, and my quads were 32". When I ssee the videos now, it's crazy. I looked like someone had sculpted my body out of clay. Even Robin marveled that my muscles were so round and perfect that I looked like a cartoon character. "You're the human Popeye!" he'd tease. "Want some spinach, my man?"

At the peak of my bodybuilding career in 1997, I really did feel like a comic-book character—one of those guys with the ridiculously round biceps, tiny waist, and bulging legs. Friends said that I should have my own action figure or superhero comic. Yet when Robin tried to get me contracts with Nike and Adidas, he was told that I was too big and muscular. I found it disappointing and a tad surreal. Here I was trying to get athletic companies to sign me when I was at the height of my physical abilities, and I still wasn't good enough. Wouldn't Nike's slogan "Just Do It" certainly apply to me? I mean, who did "it" more than I did?

Actual athletes were more encouraging, especially Arnold Schwarzenegger. Way back in 1993 when I won the Arnold Classic for the first time, he took a bunch of photos with me. I remember joking with him about my prize money. "Hey, can I cash this check tomorrow? Is it any good?"

He laughed and told the reporters, "Trust me, my checks are always good!"

In 1997, when I won his show again, Arnold came onstage and announced: "Flex Wheeler is the best bodybuilder in the history of bodybuilding." As I mentioned before, that was a mind-boggling thing for me to hear. From that point on, Arnold always said I was the best, which I'm sure was a tough thing for him to say. When he first started, everyone said that *he* was the best in the history of the sport, and he still truly loves bodybuilding—to the point that he puts on a yearly competition that allows other athletes a way to make a decent living. To put it simply, he's the best—as a man, an athlete, and an inspiration.

In fact, Arnold got really peeved that I couldn't get an endorsement deal after winning his competitions four times in a row. And he and I got to know each other well enough so that it was like two old friends reconnecting whenever we'd run into each other around Los Angeles. Arnold would even go out of his way to say hello to me. For example, one day I was at the downtown L.A. Nike store with Rico when we saw Arnold canvassing the aisles with his kids. I still felt like that shy kid from Fresno, so I brushed Rico off when he practically pushed me to go up to Arnold and say hello. "Yeah, but he's talking to someone else," I said.

"Flex, you won his show four times," Rico stated. "Go up and talk to him *now!*"

"I'm not going to bother the dude," I said.

A few minutes later, I was in the checkout line when I heard a booming Austrian voice ricochet off the walls. "Flex! How are you doing, my man?! Did that check ever clear from my last Classic?"

Rico was out of his mind with joy, but I tried to keep it casual. "Oh, hey, Arnold. I didn't see you," I said. "I'm fine. How are you?"

"What are you doing here?" Arnold asked, as if we were just two regular guys having a little conversation about shopping.

I replied, "Oh, I'm just buying some new shoes."

As I handed the cashier my Visa card, Arnold stepped in. "Oh my God! What are you doing?!" he yelled, grabbing my credit card back from the startled cashier.

"I'm, uh, buying some shoes, Arnold," I repeated.

"You have to *buy* them? *Really?* Nike isn't giving them to you for free?" Arnold then looked at the cashier with laser-hard eyes and asked, "Why does he have to pay?"

The poor girl was baffled. "Um, he has to pay because everyone does, Mr. Schwarzenegger," she timidly responded.

"No! He is one of the best bodybuilders in the world. Do you know who this guy is?" Arnold continued, and the cashier shook her head. "He's Flex Wheeler," Arnold said, triumphantly.

Soon managers were scurrying out from the back. "Is anything wrong, Mr. S?" they asked. After all, this was *Arnold Schwarzenegger*, and he was clearly unhappy. If this had been a movie, the body count would have been in the double digits.

"This guy should not be paying to wear your stuff," Arnold continued. "*You* should pay *him!*"

"Give him whatever he wants," the manager told the cashier, repeating Arnold's words. "This is Flex Wheeler, one of the best body-builders in the world."

I was dumbfounded, and Rico was almost dancing down the aisles. "Arnold," I began, "I can't—"

"Whatever he wants," the store manager repeated.

"Thanks, Arnold," I finally said.

"Oh, you can put my clothes on Mr. Wheeler's credit card," Arnold joked, plopping down a cartload of merchandise on the counter.

Everyone burst out laughing, including Rico, who by now looked like he had died and gone to heaven. He finally understood the out-of-body experience I'd had the night of the accident, because he was having one of his own.

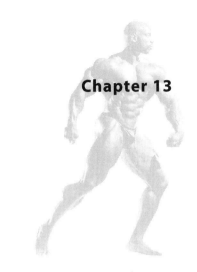

Chapter 13

Love and War

I'd like to paint a picture of the bodybuilding world as one in which everyone is as supportive as Arnold Schwarzenegger. Yeah, that would be a nice lie. The truth is that bodybuilders love to build themselves up as they knock each other down. I got into many verbal confrontations at competitions over the years. I even came close to blows with a few guys, but thankfully, one of us always had the presence of mind to step away. And I'm not happy to report that I encouraged these confrontations—I fed off them because there was an angry spot in me that needed to stir things up.

One of my most well-known disputes happened with another bodybuilder (who shall remain nameless) who accused me of having calf implants. "Flex, you fucking suck, and you shouldn't be beating me. I know you had implants," he spat out. He even took it as far as bad-mouthing me to a sports magazine, which bothered me immensely because now his accusations were in black and white. The simple truth is that knocking me boosted his reputation. People began saying, "This guy must be really tough because he's daring to talk trash about Flex."

A few months after his comments ran, I confronted Mr. Bigmouth before a competition, asking him, "Why don't you stand up and show all of us how tough you really are?" I challenged him to step outside and take it anyplace he wanted to go. I was so enraged that several other builders had to pick me up (not easy) and carry me (almost impossible) out of the room.

At which point, Mr. Mouth yelled, "Go ahead and hit me. *I* don't fight, my lawyers do—and they'll sue your ass if you put one finger on me."

I began bucking wildly against the guys carrying me, not caring if he sued me for everything I owned, because I knew that pounding him to a pulp would feel so good.

"Flex, calm down," said one of my friends. "Don't let him get to you."

But the moron kept talking, and his jaw kept moving for weeks afterwards. It got so bad that I was having visions of severely hurting this guy. I wanted to walk up to him while he was signing his photos and knock him out cold. I was so sick with fury that I tried to figure out ways to actually accomplish this little revenge scenario.

One night when I was in New York for a show, these wicked thoughts started to scare me. In fact, I got so tired of feeling that white-hot anger that I did something unusual for me: I dropped to my knees and prayed to God to help me get over it. What happened next sort of shocked me—I stood up, and I immediately felt less angry. I went home from the show the next night feeling a little lighter, and I realized that this finger-pointing wasn't my problem, it was his. I didn't want to seek revenge on someone who was so pathetic. I even felt a little bit sorry for this whacked-out loser who had to feed off other people's reputations just to make a name for himself. Did I want to talk it out with him over dinner? Hell, no. But I no longer wanted to beat him to death, so I figured that this was progress. It amazed me that all this was accomplished from one tiny prayer.

I wish I could tell you that a switch was flipped and my dark days were over, but some of the lowest times I ever had took place during this period of my life. I was living with Madeline, but I was a horrible womanizer. Girls were coming on to me day and night, and when opportunity knocked, I kept opening the door. It was weird the way these girls would just appear—before, during, and after shows. They were outside (and inside!) the guys' locker room at the gym, elevating being a groupie to a full-time job with overtime.

It was a simple deal: The girls were the supply, and a bunch of sweaty guys in a gym certainly provided the demand. I figured that secretly messing around with these girls from time to time didn't mean anything—they were just recreation, but I *loved* Madeline. The guilt was overwhelming, however, because Madeline didn't know. She never even suspected because she loved and trusted me so much. This made me feel worse. I also lived in fear that she'd find out and walk out of my life forever—and I didn't think I could make it without her.

I'd start to feel suicidal again, and I'd pull out my gun and fire it in the house. Or I'd jump into one of my cars in the middle of the night and speed down the highway at 150 miles an hour, which was the height of stupidity since I'd just barely recovered from an accident that had almost left me paralyzed.

As 1997 passed before my eyes, I figured that I'd better get something on track, so I started with my personal life. I stopped cold with the other girls, and then I sat Madeline down and told her about some of my "extracurricular activities." Let me just say that the next few weeks weren't easy—through our tears, Madeline and I had some of the most serious discussions ever about trust and fidelity, which were two areas that I had little experience in. Without betraying her confidence, let me just say that this woman must have loved me a lot, because *I* would have walked out the door had the shoe been on the other foot. Again, she chose to stay, and through her anger and grief, something surprising surfaced: *love*. I finally learned what that word really meant.

My heart could only think of one way to show Madeline how I was feeling, so one night I came home and sat her down on the bed. "Honey, I want to show you something," I said. Slowly, I took off my shoes and socks. She thought I was getting romantic, which I was, but not the way she thought. I told her, "Look at this tattoo I got." I pulled up my pant leg, and there it was: MADELINE WHEELER, in full color, right on my ankle.

Her eyes popped when she read it.

"Will you marry me?" I asked with a huge grin.

Now it's a good thing she said yes—my woman has a pretty long name, so there was a lot of pain involved with this proposal. But the minute Madeline saw the tattoo, she began to giggle hysterically. And then, in her most concerned voice, she asked, "Honey, did it hurt?"

I milked the moment, trying to sound like a torture victim. "Yeah, it hurt really, really bad. It's not like your name is Sue. So you better marry me now."

She started to cry and said yes.

Just before the wedding, I won the Ironman Pro for the fourth time. I felt bad for the other guys because I was flying so high that I just knew I was going to win. It wasn't personal or vindictive for me, and I even admired my fellow competitors that year. We were all singing the same song but doing it a little differently. I admired their techniques, and honestly rooted for them while they tried their best. I dedicated my first-place trophy to Madeline and announced our engagement onstage. It was a big day for me.

But on June 28, 1997, the *real* big day arrived when I got married. My entire family flew from Fresno to Madeline's hometown of San Jose. We had this beautiful, extravagant church wedding, and I blubbered like a big old baby when my beautiful bride walked down the aisle in a dress her sister's mother-in-law (who was a seamstress) made for her. Madeline had fallen in love with this $4,000 dress she saw in a magazine, and I was dying to buy it for her, but she thought it would mean more if a family member made the dress by hand. It turned out even better than the one in the picture, and Madeline looked like an angel in it.

Robin was my best man, and Rico was a groomsman—and knowing me all too well, they had plenty of tissues in their pockets for me. My only disappointment was that my grandmother couldn't be there, but I knew she was there in spirit, and one day the two most important women in my life would finally meet.

As Madeline and I said our vows, I looked into her stunning face and realized that most other women would have bailed out of a relationship with me given all the challenges (to put it mildly). I couldn't believe that she'd chosen to stick to me like glue. She saw things in me that I couldn't even recognize in myself, and perhaps I had a few surprises left that she had yet to see. But no matter what, she had enough steel to embrace whatever the future held.

Hey, enough of this mush. The reception was the best party of my life. People I hadn't seen in more than 15 years showed up, and Ed Conners, a legendary bodybuilder, made a toast. Madeline looked ridiculously beautiful, even when I stepped on her feet on the dance floor.

While Madeline was getting her toes crushed, Robin took the white roses from the church and put them all over our honeymoon suite—including the king-sized bed. The next day, we left for Cancun for a blow-out honeymoon, which, by the way, was a total surprise to Madeline. When Robin picked us up the next morning in a big Suburban packed with gifts, he pretended like we were just driving home. When he took us to the airport instead, she was stunned (much to my delight).

I probably didn't pack the right clothes for my new bride, but who cared? We got burned by the sun by day and spent the nights making love while the tropical breezes floated in the windows. Life seemed perfect . . . and at least for a little while, it was.

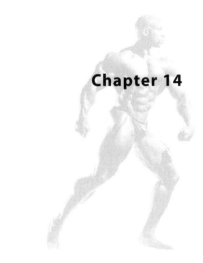

Chapter 14

The Fame Game

As I trained at Gold's Gym in late 1997, I was surrounded by top-notch athletes, world-class movie stars, billionaires, and babes. I was also constantly hounded by fans and wannabe hangers-on. The fact that little Kenny Wheeler *had* fans was incredible, yet these people were as pushy as those who follow Madonna or Bruce Springsteen. It got to the point where the gym's management had to step in and keep other patrons away from me so I could get my workout done. I had work to do, and I needed some silence.

The autograph-seekers (especially the ladies) were flattering, but it was too easy to let them mess with my head. I was at Gold's to concentrate, which wasn't easy when some D-cup gym hottie would lean over my workout bench and want me to sign her fake breasts. But if I had some free time, I'd lift up a pen and sign "To my best friend, Yolanda, who I've never met before this moment."

It was amusing . . . and I figured that the money I was making made up for the inconvenience. My endorsement deals had finally come through again, which meant that Madeline and I were able to move to a lush house in a gated community in Los Angeles. It was 26,000 square feet and crazy beautiful, and every single night when

I'd walk around the grounds—yes, I had grounds—I'd get this feeling that security was going to come around and eject me. This couldn't be *my* house or *my* beautiful woman waiting for me inside. It seemed like at any moment the alarm clock would ring and someone would yell, "Wake up! It's time to go back to work at the jail!" But, incredibly, it was no dream.

The money poured in, and I let it seep back out just as quickly (which would later become a major mistake). What did I know back then? You'd have thought that I would have learned from my accident, but I put all that right out of my mind. I was living large—I couldn't buy enough cars, jewelry, or expensive furniture. My new hobby was rampage shopping sprees, despite the advice of Robin, who begged me to save my money for a day when my body wouldn't cooperate anymore. Screw that—I felt like I'd earned these spoils, especially when I was suffering through those hours on the treadmill each day. I'd be miserable, yet I'd will my legs to pump harder and faster. Sometimes I'd remember that scene in *Rocky II* when all the kids ran after Sly while he was doing his cardio down the streets of Philly. I wondered what would happen if *I* ran down a street in the middle of L.A. I'd probably have some muggers running after me . . . although that wasn't a bad training plan. I imagined how fast I'd have to go to ditch them and protect my diamond-studded Rolex.

The possessions helped me feel even larger, but strangely, they didn't make me happier. I had three Mercedes E300s, two Mercedes SL500s, four BMWs, a couple of sport-utility vehicles, and a Porsche convertible. But if I drove to the gym in one of them, I'd still be miserable. I'd pull into a parking lot and someone would yell, "Nice wheels, man!" I couldn't just say "Thanks"— instead I had to give off attitude. "What's it to you?" I'd fire back.

I'd turn around the next day and trade the car in for a newer model, never once thinking about the tremendous amounts of money I was shelling out on stupid whims. I tried to buy the happiness that seemed to elude me, but I still carried around the demons of a 14-year-old boy who felt he wasn't worthy of anything.

Somewhere along the way, those demons really started to unleash themselves at competitions. I didn't visualize myself the way other people saw me. They'd say, "Fantastic!"; I'd say, "Passable." I'd pick up

My Grandmommy and
angel, Ethel Pearl Wheeler.

Sharalene, Darnell, and
me. Of course, I'm the
one who's crying.

My first bodybuilding
competition. Note that
I'm wearing my under-
wear as posing trunks.

Me in high school thinking
I'm hot stuff. Check out
those biceps and my first
good pair of leather pants.

Here's what I looked like when
I placed fifth at the Nationals
in 1989. I knew it wouldn't be
long before I was number one.

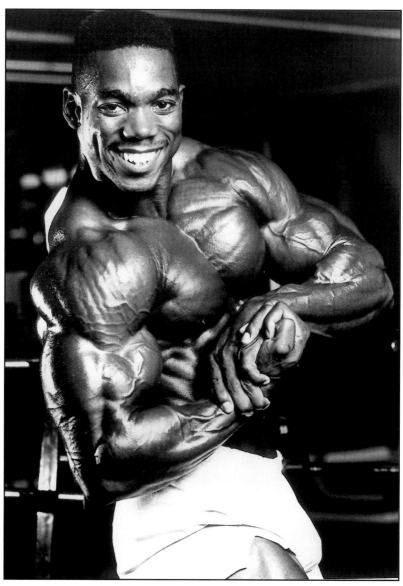

"And the winner of the 1989 Mr. California contest is
Flex Wheeler!"

Who are these two handsome dudes? Rico and I
prove that we're cool cats for the camera in 1990.

Back in the day. I'm training with Rico [top] and
Chris Cormier [right].

Winning the 1992 Nationals
made me smile and then cry.

Who would have ever
thought that the poor
kid from Fresno who
slept with cockroaches
would be hired to
guest-pose in front of
the Taj Mahal? It even
blows *my* mind!

I'm posing for my trainer Charles Glass prior to winning the 1996 Night of the Champions. That look on my face says, "Baby, you better watch out!"

Maybe success went to my head . . . *nah!*

One of my biggest fans has always been my sister, Sharalene. I love you, sis.

Celebrating Christmas 1996 with the most beautiful woman on the planet—Madeline.

It was one of the happiest nights of my life when Arnold Schwarzenegger told me that I'd won the Arnold Classic in 1997.

This is the back that was created by God . . .
and a lot of hours in the gym.

The real prize after a serious competition is an extra-large cheese pizza with about 100 toppings. I'm saying, "This is my pie. Order yourself another one, 'cause I'm not sharing."

Cha-ching! It's always nice to get a check for $100,000, which is what I hauled in for winning the Arnold Classic in 1997.

I will love, honor, and cherish Madeline forever. Here we are
on our wedding day, with [left to right], her father, Paul;
her mom, Janet; my mom, Gloria; and my father, Webster.

My new bride and I on our wonderful
honeymoon in Cancun, Mexico.

I couldn't resist
putting in one
more photo of
Madeline looking
like the bomb.

On the road again. At a United States Army base in Japan,
I met with the men and women who keep this country
safe and sound. They'll always have my utmost respect.

Prior to the 1999 Olympia,
I took up more space in
my bedroom than most of
the furniture.

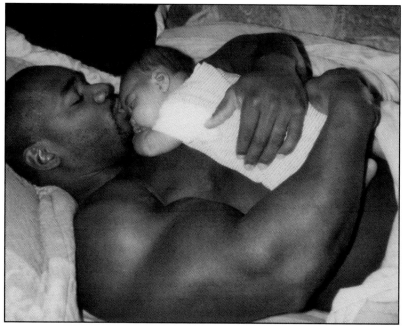

"I see great things for this little man." Here's my new son, Darius, who finds Daddy's big chest to be a comfy king-sized bed.

My son Kennen at age 10. Look at that bicep shape—he's just like his dad!

It amazes me how such a petite woman like Madeline can lift me off the floor when I'm exhausted from training. No wonder she's so toned!

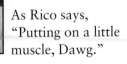

As Rico says, "Putting on a little muscle, Dawg."

Look at that happy family! The beautiful girl in my
arms is our baby daughter, Nia. Meanwhile, Darius
wants Daddy to get up and play.

At a seminar after the 2002 Mr. Olympia with Lee Priest.

I'm working at home, planning my next move, which is
to train as a clean athlete and spread the word.

As Madeline, Darius, Nia, and I celebrate
Christmas in 2002, I can only count my blessings and
thank God that I'm here with my babies.

some photo of myself in a champion pose, and start picking it apart, muscle by muscle. When I look back now at the videos of myself in 1997, I can only say that I'm astonished at that body. It doesn't seem as if it could have belonged to *me,* but I know that it's the same form I tucked into bed every night.

Life improved in ways other than the financial aspect. My eight-year-old son, Kennen, visited often. My wide neck would stretch out to kiss his little head, and when he'd giggle, I'd tell him, "I love you so much! When you're 40 and I'm an old geezer, I'll still be kissing you!"

I was in constant contact with Brandy, who was almost 18. I sounded very fatherly as I'd insist, "If you need anything, you call me first. And you better stay away from boys—they're beasts!"

My big fingers also dialed my father's number on a frequent basis, and he was out of his mind with pride. "At the Walgreens, somebody came up and asked me, 'Is that your son on the cover of that magazine?'" I'd just grin.

On one phone call, however, he sounded serious, and I was worried. "What's the matter, Daddy?"

"Oh, Kenny," his voice cracked, "I wasn't there for you as a little boy. I just want you to know that I always loved you, but I just didn't know how to handle things."

"Handling things is hard," I reassured him. I forgave my dad for the past, but I never had the courage to mention what had happened with his girlfriend, Crystal. Why make him feel even worse?

As for the rest of my family, every once in a while I'd walk out of the gym and my tired legs would suddenly get a burst of energy because Darnell was there in the parking lot, leaning up against my nice car and incurring the wrath of the security guards. "Hey, little brother," he'd say, and I didn't mind his ass print on my ride. We'd hug and catch up, although I never got the full story of his life. "I'm surviving," he'd tell me, and I had a sinking feeling that there was more going on than he wanted to share with me. Later, I'd find out that I was right. . . .

Most important, my mammoth legs carried me across the lawn to catch Madeline, who was often the victim of my inept use of our new $10,000 sprinkler system. "Flex, now I'm soaking wet!" she'd scream.

I'd bust out laughing. "Honey, where I grew up we had one green hose, not an underground sprinkling system, or whatever this thing is here. But you look so cute when you're mad," I'd tell her, dripping wet myself.

(⊶)

Back when I had it all in my grasp, my smile reeked confidence, but my mind feared that I somehow didn't deserve my life. That's why a lot of the time I came off as an arrogant champion, and the press painted me as one extra-large pain in the ass. What they didn't know is that I was completely intimidated and nervous whenever I was in public. Looking at my massive form, no one would have thought for a second that those insecurities were true, but I've read that a lot of extremely outgoing actors and performers say that in reality, they're scared to go onstage and all their bravado is just a shield. Let's just say that I can relate.

At competitions, my hard eyes and habit of walking onstage with my fists balled up like I was ready to have an actual fight was merely a coverup for my trembling nerves. I'd look everywhere but at the crowd, so I was branded as unfriendly, and worse yet, ungrateful. Once again, this was just another defense mechanism. If people only knew what was happening to me on the inside, they might have taken me into their hearts, which would have made me feel better. Yet I wouldn't let anyone see inside of me, because that wasn't "being a man."

Despite all of this, I was perceived as a hero to many. When I think about this today, the same conclusion always hits me: People have it so backwards. Winning competitions or sinking a ball into a hoop doesn't make you great. What defines greatness is when people accept you for whatever you are at your rawest moments. I only wish I could relive my days of extreme fame, because now I'd really appreciate the fact that people willingly gave me their attention and respect. They'd wait for hours just to see me, which was a great honor they were bestowing on me.

I also wish I could tell those same people that I'm really not a hero—heroes are doctors and teachers, and *they* should get the accolades and Nike contracts. The people who go to war to make sure our kids are safe should get our cheers, make a million dollars, and live in fancy homes as a reward for their bravery. Nurses who make us feel better when we're writhing in pain should get free clothes when they want them. Instead, all of these people get pennies for their efforts and still come back day after day to do great work that goes unsung. It just doesn't seem right to me.

And what *really* isn't right is the fact that I was earning $90,000 a weekend for posing, and I complained that I wasn't happy. How can I explain this? Okay, remember *The Wizard of Oz?* You know how Dorothy and her friends thought the Wizard was this big scary dude, but when they got down to the facts, he was just some loony old guy behind a curtain? That was me. I was strong on the outside, but if you looked closer, I was really this little guy who didn't want them to pull back the curtain. My muscles, my big cars, and my huge house were just my way of pretending to be more than skinny Kenny Wheeler from Fresno—the person that I knew deep down inside I was always going to be.

There's no other way to say this, but I was a total rude-ass to people. Someone would come up and say, "Oh, Flex, I have a picture of you on my fridge, and every single time I want to cheat on my diet, I look at you for inspiration."

I'd just look at them and say, "My picture won't stop you from eating crap."

The saddest part of my whole story is that when I had a chance to be a motivating force the first time around, I took a pass. I just couldn't deal with the fact that people wanted to be like me, and I figured that anyone who felt that way needed a lobotomy. Nevertheless, these fans were everywhere. At the grocery store, I was mobbed to the point where I'd have to leave without my food. I couldn't get gas without signing a few autographs and having the whole procedure take half an hour. Of course, many people just stared from afar, because I gave off a definite "Don't bug me" vibe.

Kids were another story. I love kids—well, most of the time anyway. I remember in late 1997 I was in Beverly Hills buying yet another new car, and this little white kid kept staring at me. Finally, he shouted across the room to his mom, "Hey, it's that jock! I bet he's on steroids!"

I couldn't believe it. This was a ritzy car place in the most expensive town on Earth. I walked over to the kid and said, "You really shouldn't be so nosy—and you certainly shouldn't use words when you have no idea what they mean."

I guess seeing me slightly peeved was enough to make the kid almost wet his pants, and he practically ran out of the place. His words, however, helped form a new worry spot inside my head. It was obvious that the kid knew about steroids, because even as early as 1990, stories about these drugs and the dangers of using them had started to creep into the mainstream press. Now, it seems, I wasn't just getting "oohs" and "ahhs" from fans—I was being asked the sort of questions that were no one's business.

For example, I was once on a plane coming back from a personal appearance, and as I walked into first class, the flight attendant gasped, "Oh my God! You're so big! Do you take steroids?"

I just stared at her, but I was so embarrassed that I wanted to spontaneously evaporate. "You know," I told her, "that's really private. That's like me asking you what sexual positions you prefer!"

Placing her hands on her hips, she stammered, "How rude!"

Yes, it was rude of me, and now I'm sorry, but I guess I was getting as freaked out as everyone else about those shots and pills I'd taken daily now for more than a decade.

At the grocery store, it happened again. "Do you take steroids?" a woman asked.

"Do you swallow?" I retorted, watching as she huffed away. It was private business, and I felt degraded every single time someone brought it up. I knew that people didn't understand what it was like to be a champion bodybuilder, but why did they have to belittle me?

I did like to have fun with people, though. One time Madeline heard one of my snappy retorts. "I can't stand it when you do that sort of thing," she said.

I replied, "Honey, I just have the raunchiest and weirdest sense of humor."

I'll tell you a funny story that she hates, but maybe I'll have her skip this chapter. This middle-aged woman came up to me and said, "You're a professional football player, right?"

I told her, "No, ma'am, I'm actually in the entertainment business."

"What do you do?" she asked.

"Adult movies," I answered evenly.

"Really?" she cooed. "Any titles I've heard of or rented?"

I replied, "You may have heard of my most recent film, *Lean Black Lover.*"

She smiled and said, "Oh, yes. I think I *have* heard of it."

As she said that, Madeline appeared. The woman grinned at both of us and walked off. "That's cold-blooded, Flex," Madeline said. "Now she's going to think that I'm some porn star, too."

At least one of us got a good laugh from that one!

What I found most interesting, though, was the reaction I got from hardcore brothers on the streets. A lot of punks would try to start trouble with me because of my size, and I never took them seriously. But these guys that lived the "thug life" to the core would come up to me and say, "You know what, Flex? I really respect what you do. Keep doing it." I was always deeply touched by them, and it made me feel that I'd stereotyped these gang guys the same way people judged me without ever getting to know me.

It just goes to show you that you can never really tell what someone has going on underneath their public act. We're all actors—some of us are just better at it than others.

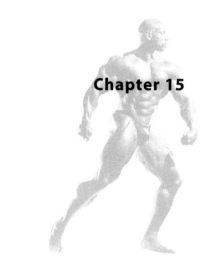

Chapter 15

Sweating It Out

At this point, I'd like to take a break and give you an up-close and personal look at what it was like to be a professional body-builder. At the height of my career, people would gaze at my body in wonder, telling me that they wished they could live in my skin for one day. Well, here's what it was like.

When I was training for competitions, I'd start the day by waking up in darkness and glaring at the moon. At 4 A.M., I'd stumble out of bed and will myself to put on four pairs of sweatpants and three sweatshirts. I didn't wear the padding as protection from the chilly morning air—it upped my perspiration, causing me to sweat gallons. I looked like a mummy when I stepped onto the treadmill that sat like a foe in the corner of my bedroom. I'd set the incline and speed dials, and groan because I knew I had a solid hour of walking as fast as humanly possible. That's 3,600 seconds of movement, and each one went by as slowly as the final hour of the last day of school.

I'd do my first hour of cardio before the birds even thought about chirping, and Madeline would generally go in the other room to go back to sleep. Many mornings I didn't even turn on the stereo or the TV—I'd just pump my legs, stare into the blackness, and listen to the silence. The clock was cruel, because I'd think that I'd knocked off 15 minutes, only to realize that it had been a measly 5. I'd will myself to hang in there: *Don't quit on yourself. Don't punk out!* Yes, I was tired, but I'd push on because I was that '70s music group come to life: I was blood. I was sweat. I was tears.

But my body—oh, my aching body. It was worse on the days when I'd wear a "sauna suit" under all those sweats, because then my entire being was wrapped in thick plastic like I was a human Thanksgiving leftover. Yet it was necessary if I was going to lose those last few crucial ounces.

As the minutes ticked on, my leg muscles would begin to scream, and I often had to stop for a few minutes or I'd pass out. *Man, don't be weak. Get back on!* I'd tell myself, and I'd keep going. After I did my "time," I'd step off the treadmill, only to find that I couldn't walk at all because there was nothing left in my legs. I'd collapse to the floor, and with my last bit of energy, I'd actually crawl to the next room to tell Madeline I was done.

Without a whimper of complaint, Madeline would pop out of bed to find her pathetic heap of a husband in a clump on the carpet. She'd get down on the floor with me and strip off my hot, smelly, sweaty clothes, because I was helpless. In those moments on the rug, I didn't feel like a champion—I felt like a dead man. When she was done peeling the wet sweats off of me, Madeline would use all her strength to help me to the shower. I've told you all how small she is, so you understand that it certainly wasn't easy for her to haul me up, let alone let me lean on her as we lurched slowly toward the bathroom.

Eventually we'd reach the shower, and Madeline would turn on the spray, which brought me instant relief. As the cool water washed the life back into me, Madeleine would head downstairs to get my food ready, timing it perfectly so that she was back to help dry me off. After walking me back to bed, she'd help me eat my breakfast, which usually consisted of a quarter cup of oatmeal and two dry chicken breasts (sometimes I got to live it up and have three quarters of a cup of rice and three chicken breasts, but if I was on a real low-carb plan, I only ate chicken).

Often I'd get to the point where I'd gag if I smelled food cooking downstairs. This meant that on many mornings, Madeline would sit there and talk me through each meal. She'd patiently remind me that my head was playing games and the next move was mine to win. Still, I'd sit there and struggle through each bite, chewing extra slowly.

"Just a few bites now," Madeline would say.

After I'd get through my breakfast, she'd move the dishes away, and we'd usually curl up under the covers again until I had to do the next session. What? You thought that was it? I wish! We'd have to go through this torture every three hours, six or seven times a day, because that was just part of the fun when I was in training.

At 10 A.M., I'd kiss my wife good-bye, and then I'd drive an hour to the gym to train for two and a half hours, topped by another hour of cardio on the treadmill. Next, I'd eat the same tasteless food that I'd had for breakfast, and I'd finish up in the posing room by going through the mandatory bodybuilding positions.

After driving another hour home, I'd be too tired to get out of the car, so I'd just blow the horn. Madeline would race out to meet me and help me out. She'd let me lean on her until we were inside, where she'd peel the clothes off me again, leaving a puddle of sweat at my feet.

At these moments, strange thoughts would go through my head. I'd heard of wrestlers and football players dying from overexertion, and I'd wonder if I could make it through all of this. I knew that I had to drink another gallon of water, because the more you take out, the more you must put in. Reminding myself that dehydrated athletes tended to die, I forced myself to gulp it down. I should admit that I've passed out a number of times during and after a workout because I'd get so hot and tired that I really couldn't take another breath. I'd feel the world going fuzzy, only to wake up minutes later wondering if anyone had seen me pass out. We champions don't think about our lives—we only concern ourselves with what it looks like to the outside world.

In the sanctuary of our home, my wife had seen it all. In our early married days, she didn't mind that I couldn't talk much as she dragged me upstairs into another shower and then into bed. A few hours later, I'd have to force down another disgusting meal, go back to the gym, have another breast of chicken, and spend another hour driving home. This was bodybuilding at the champion level, and it wasn't pretty or glamorous. In a nutshell, training for a show was nothing short of trying to kill myself, which was ironic for someone who had always been suicidal.

On top of the backbreaking physical schedule I had to keep, being as big as I was caused a lot of problems in my day-to-day life. For instance, I could be having a conversation with someone and instantly fall asleep because my size guaranteed a lack of oxygen. When I went to bed at night, I needed to put body pillows between my legs or the circulation would be cut off; I'd also have to snuggle another pillow between my arms or I could cut off the blood flow to my chest cavity and stop my heart.

The most difficult thing was just standing around. I often made other people nervous since I was always shifting my feet. This wasn't a jittery habit or some dance step I was working on—I simply couldn't stand on one leg for very long because it hurt my hips and my waist. My thighs would begin to tremble and ache, while at the same time, my legs would become so tense that they'd involuntarily begin flexing. So I usually stood with my legs wide open, looking like John Wayne after he'd spent a few days riding the range. Walking meant kicking my legs out, and I guess I never realized how funny this looked until I saw Kennen and some of the neighborhood kids start to mimic me.

Making love? Well, it was tough but not impossible. Enough said, or Madeline will certainly kill me. Yes, she's a little thing, but I know enough not to mess around here. After all, you can probably tell that she's emerged as the real tough one in our family.

Okay, driving is a safe subject, although it was another challenge for me. Big cars were an absolute requirement, which is why I'd always buy the largest Mercedes or BMWs. Sure, I liked the luxury and amenities in these cars, but most of all I could actually squeeze myself into the driver's seat. A Mazda Miata or Honda Civic? Please. I'd have needed one for each leg. And I couldn't ride bicycles with Madeline because they didn't make one that could hold me up.

One of the worst things in my life was trying to go the bathroom on a commercial airline, and I found out that the skies were not so friendly for a man my size. I always tried to avoid liquids when I flew, no matter how thirsty I was. I just couldn't face the so-called accommodations.

One Sunday, Madeline really wanted to get away, so we went to Magic Mountain (an amusement park in Southern California). It sounded like so much fun, but neither of us realized that she'd be alone on every single ride due to the simple fact that I couldn't fit into any of them. I managed to squeeze myself into one of the roller-coaster cars, which wasn't a good idea, to say the least. I couldn't handle breathing, because my organs were pressed so tightly in that little metal seat that I thought my tonsils were going to pop out, and I almost fainted.

My beautiful new wife grabbed my hand, and in her most worried voice said, "Flex, you look gray to me. Maybe we should get a doctor, or at least pass on the Hurl-and-Whirl ride."

"No, no," I rasped. "I'll . . . be . . . okay. Just give me a minute to get my breath. 'Cause honey, this is so [gasp] fun!"

Another time, I tried to go outside and play basketball with two friends. I lost my breath to the point that I actually saw little white stars in front of my eyes. I had to give the ball away and sit down on the sidelines, which was humiliating for a professional athlete. Then it dawned on me that I'd chosen a life where there were only two options: compete . . . or do something different.

I was one of the most successful bodybuilders of all time, but I was starting to think that soon I'd have to redefine my priorities.

Chapter 16

Discovering a New World

In 1998, I continued my quest to buy happiness. On a whim, I bought an even bigger home in the posh Los Angeles suburb of Rowland Heights—a 48,000 square-foot spread of happiness that included a six-car garage, winding driveway, and enough palm trees to populate a small desert island. I felt like I was living in some sort of fairy tale where the prince gets the girl, the castle, and the cool sports cars.

That year I came in first at the Arnold Classic and copped a second at Mr. Olympia, which was disappointing because I was once again just points away from winning. But instead of letting it get to me, I pushed even harder. I still had something to prove, and I wouldn't be stopped.

One day Robin told me that an international sports group wanted me to make personal appearances in Africa. I was a little scared because I'd heard so many bad things about how people, especially African-American men, were treated in South Africa. For the first time in a very long while, I was concerned about my safety.

It's funny how your expectations about a situation and the reality of it are often miles apart. As soon as I got there, I was almost blinded by the most beautiful sunset of my life, and a strange calm came over me. The homeland of my ancestors turned out to be a stunning place—when I wasn't posing, I'd take six- or seven-hour drives into the wilderness to watch elephants walking in pairs and lions running wild and free in the distance. Not once did I feel afraid out there.

This experience made me realize how TV only shows you the worst parts of a place and never its magical qualities. I guess it's easier to glorify the bad stuff rather than embrace what's so amazing that you can't even put it into words. Africa did have its hazards, though. When I drove through the mountain ranges, I had to be really careful, because on each side of the narrow roads were drop-offs so steep that I couldn't see where they ended. But I loved that it was so primitive, with no freeways . . . and no telephone lines. I found out that the natives steal the phone lines for the copper in them, which they sell, so it's easier for the government to confine phone usage to the towns. That seems like an inconvenience, but imagine the sheer freedom of not being linked to anyone for a few days. It was like being on another planet—a strangely peaceful one.

Some of the cities proved to be a challenge. I found out that South Africa is the carjacking capital of the world. Robbers are notorious for just walking up to someone on the streets, waving a gun, and calmly saying, "Give me everything you have." Because of that, *everyone* walks around armed—gun ownership is easy and legal, and people don't even conceal their weapons. That's why I didn't balk at the three armed guards who flanked me everywhere, even at interviews.

I felt bad for some of the fans, especially the ones who couldn't get close to me. These were people who faced poverty so severe that it was beyond anything I'd experienced in my own childhood. They didn't know where their next meal was coming from, and I figured that if they could feed off the presence of a visiting sports star and it made them happy for even one minute, then I'd done my job. I only wished that I could have reached out and touched them, because I knew we'd all remember the encounter forever.

One fan told me that he'd had a lucky week because, for once, the power lines hadn't been overloaded. I guess the electricity can be shut off for weeks until someone climbs a tower and risks being shocked to death in order to turn it back on. The young man told me that nights can be quite frightening without light. I vowed to never complain about anything once I got back home.

It inspired me that the people of Africa didn't bemoan their fate. I found that they just wanted to make things better for the next generation, which proved to me that people are the same everywhere. I felt honored just being in their presence. Even though we didn't speak the same language, they accepted and respected me, which is what every single one of us wants—no matter if we're straight or gay, black or white, champion bodybuilder or skinny kid from Fresno. We all just want to be embraced for who we are, and in Africa, I found that love and acceptance.

Around the same time, I was offered very lucrative deals to tour other foreign countries, so I jumped at the chance to do so. I went to Russia, which was freezing and snowy all the time. Not that I'm here to give you travel tips, but if you're ever planning on touring the Ukraine, do yourself a favor and pack some long, fur-lined underwear. This was a severe place in more ways than one, and it freaked me out that everywhere I went, I saw these huge old-fashioned school buses filled with armed guards caressing their AK-47s. I had to pass through many a checkpoint in order to appear at gyms that were dingy and dark hellholes filled with rusty old equipment. The people were very polite, although they rarely smiled. But I loved that when I signed a photo, their hard faces would break into a grin.

When I was in Moscow, a guard wanted my autograph, and I asked him if I could hold his gun for a minute. I'm not sure what "Are you kidding?" sounds like in Russian, but that's what he seemed to be saying. In the end, I didn't get to touch the weapon, but hopefully I touched the hearts of a few of the people who'd never met a bodybuilder before in their lives.

At one of the bodybuilding competitions in Moscow, I pulled up to the historic opera house where the show was being held and couldn't believe that there was a line of people stretched around the building—I mean, it was 30-below zero with ice raining from the sky!

The translator told me that many of these folks had traveled for two days to get to the competition, and a lot of them had made the journey just because they'd heard that I was appearing. It broke my heart to hear that these men and women had come so far in such extreme conditions to shake my hand or have me sign a photo. I also realized that some of the fans couldn't even afford tickets to come inside—they'd made the trek just to catch a glimpse of me getting out of a car. Against the advice of everyone, I hopped out of the limo, holding my photos tightly in one hand. The translators and sponsors of the show went ballistic because their plan was to sell these photos. I didn't care. I started giving them away to those who'd have to choose between having a meal or getting a picture of me.

I stood in a snow bank outside this opera house and began to get mobbed by the fans, but it wasn't frightening. In fact, what happened next was a true high. One young man pointed at my L.A. Lakers baseball cap, which was one of about 20 I had at home. I'd forgotten it was even on my head—and then it dawned on me. I asked him, "You want my hat?"

He nodded and began to cry, so I immediately whipped the thing off and gave it to him. What he did next humbled me to the core: He took off his winter jacket and gave it to me. It was the type of coat that was only issued to Russian athletes, and I really did want it as a souvenir, but I wouldn't have been able to live with myself if I'd taken it outright. As he stood there shivering with his arms across his chest, I slipped 500 American dollars into his hands. "Buy another coat, son," I said. To this day, his jacket means more to me than any Mercedes. It reminds me how some things, like sports, can break down any barrier.

A few months later, I made a pit stop in Kuwait, which I'd thought was the poorest spot on Earth. Man, did I find out I was wrong! I was told that more rich people lived in this small country than anyplace else on Earth. Even the mall I went to was filled with stores like Chanel, Versace, Movado, and other swanky names I couldn't even pronounce.

"After shopping, we will take you for a camel ride," said one of my handlers. I took a pass on that one, preferring to ride on wheels.

Speaking of which, the cars were great. Every single one was a Lamborghini, Hummer, Ferrari, or Lincoln. *Every single car!* It was just unbelievable.

I mentioned that I needed to go to a gym for a quick workout, and the next thing I knew, a red twin-turbo Ferrari pulled up in front of my hotel. Inside was this 25-year-old kid who jumped out to furiously pump my hand. Omar's first words to me were: "Want a ride?"

He flipped me the keys, actually trusting me with a car that cost more than many people's homes in America. When I came back two hours later, Omar said, "I'm such a fan of yours that after your workout, it would be an honor for me to show you my home."

I smiled and said, "Sure! Thanks, bro."

Omar's home was a three-story palace with two huge golden doors and high-tech surveillance equipment. I walked around shaking my head in amazement. "What do you do?" I asked him.

"Oh, I'm in college," he said. "But my father is the third most powerful lawyer in the country." He also told me that when a couple gets married in Kuwait, the government gives them a ridiculous amount of money.

I suddenly felt that offering this kid tickets to my show seemed like a moot point, and I was right.

"Oh, I had front-row seats, but I gave them away because I have to study tonight," he said.

That floored me, so I said, "I have so much respect for you, Omar." I mean, here was this kid who was incredibly wealthy *and* he'd been waiting hours to meet me, but he was willing to sacrifice going to the show because he wanted to give himself and his new wife the very best life he could. I said, "You go study, bro. I'm proud of you. You've got the right idea."

Omar smiled. "But Flex, all you have is a lonely hotel room," he said. "I'd be honored if you'd stay here with me."

"How will I get to my show?" I asked.

"Oh, you could take my Ferrari, or one of my friends can loan you his Lamborghini," said the kid, who had the ultimate plan cooking in his mind. "We'll just line up the two cars in the driveway with the keys in them, and you can choose whichever one you want."

Naturally I took him up on his offer. I chose to drive the Ferrari, and when I returned, I showed Omar a bunch of poses. He even insisted that I call Madeline—imagine that phone bill! I told the kid that he had a spare room in case he ever came to Los Angeles, and he's visited me several times. We've remained friends for years, which proves that if you just open your mind and heart, wonderful surprises can be found everywhere, especially where you least expect them. (But I'll go on record to say that I never opened my mind to that whole camel-riding stuff. A man does have his limits.)

Back at home, Madeline and I were working on having a baby. We were diligently trying, and let me just say that I was giving this 100 percent of my effort and attention. Meanwhile, I continued to pose and win—thousands of dollars poured into my bank account, but I was hitting the wall from exhaustion. I could have gone on to do other competitions, but I was zoned out from the wedding, the baby making, and the travel. I felt like the Lakers at the end of a long championship season.

The sports columnists called me the best bodybuilder in history. I had a beautiful house, an incredible wife, and yes, a baby on the way. I just wanted to enjoy it for a while, but suddenly I felt so tired that I felt like I could sleep for a year. That's when it dawned on me that something was horribly wrong.

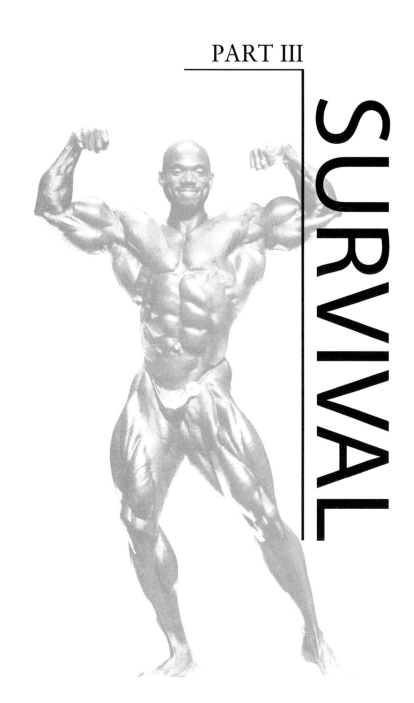

PART III

SURVIVAL

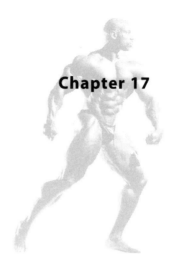

Chapter 17

Running on Miracles

I've saved this part for now because I didn't want to be a downer, but I'm sure you've been wondering what effects a decade-plus of steroid use has had on my system. Let me just say that there are no easy rides in life. You always pay the toll, even if it's years later.

It's interesting that my first serious health problems stemmed from taking diuretics, not steroids. It's no secret that bodybuilders commonly pop as many of these as possible before a show, because the pills drain all of the water out of the body. The resulting effect onstage is a body with every muscle and vein popping out—it looks cut and chiseled to the max.

This quick fix isn't the least bit healthy, however. Our organs, especially the kidneys, need liquid flowing through them at all times or they'll shut down. And once the kidneys have quit, there's no going back—it can mean dialysis or even death.

I don't pass around any blame when it comes to my steroid and diuretic use. During my years as a champion bodybuilder, it was expected that I'd do whatever was necessary to win. But it was in 1992 that I first found out that all this stress on my system could turn ugly. Here's what happened.

I'd just won the USA Championship, so my friends Rico and Chris and I went to the Cheesecake Factory restaurant in Los Angeles to celebrate with some burritos and strawberry cheesecake. Training was over, and I was never an angel in the food department (when I didn't have to worry about being under the eye of a judge).

We sat down at the table, and I felt like a Mack truck had smashed into my stomach. All my muscles started cramping profusely in my midsection like a vice was squeezing me from the inside out. "My legs!" I cried, as the muscles in them began to tremble violently.

"Oh my God, Flex!" Chris said, running to my side with some ice water.

I couldn't even move my hand to grasp the glass, but Rico knew what was happening. I was simply so dehydrated that my kidneys were failing right there in the Cheesecake Factory. He and Chris carried me out of the restaurant so that we could go home. Then, believe it or not, the pain stopped and my muscles quieted down.

I closed my eyes in relief, and a few minutes later, I told the boys, "Hey, I didn't really want Cheesecake Factory anyway. Let's go get a pizza."

I was about to dig into a deep-dish pie when I felt the cramping begin again. It was less severe, so this time I just gutted it out. Honestly, I didn't want to worry anyone, but what I didn't know at the time is that I could have just dropped over and died with *my next bite.*

I'd played Russian roulette with my health for many years because I was young and strong and felt invincible. In 1993, I injured my back training, and the doctors in my life were singing the same depressing song: "Flex, you can't go to Europe to compete. We won't allow it."

You might have guessed that I'm no good at following directions when they keep me away from competitions. I told Rico, "There's no way I'm not going to the next show."

He nodded, knowing that this was nonnegotiable.

After spending ten hours on a plane to Germany, my back was in so much pain that my first stop was to a local doc. Before I knew what was happening, he turned me over and gave me a shot in my spine. "Don't move," he said in broken English.

"Shit! It hurts! What did you do?" I screamed.

"Don't move," he repeated. "You could be paralyzed if you do."

I sat still for the next 20 minutes, breaking out in a cold sweat either from the shot or the fear—I couldn't tell which was worse. I couldn't believe it when he told me, "If you would have moved half an inch more when I inserted that needle, you would have never walked again."

Was this enough to make me appreciate the blood pumping through my veins and the muscles that lifted me to great heights? Nah. Backstage at the Arnold Classic in 1995, I started cramping really bad again, but this time the pain made my experience at the Cheesecake Factory look like a walk in the park. My abdominal muscles began to tense until they became a huge, angry, pulsating knot. The pain made me dizzy and blind at the same time, and I prayed for it to stop. As soon as my stomach stopped hurting, my leg muscles started to jump up like they were going AWOL, and my back muscles began rippling like waves on the ocean.

Madeline and my crew watched in horror, because it's not every day that an athlete's muscles contract about 1,000 times harder than he can make them during a workout. It looked like my body was being possessed by the devil. At one point, I thought my arm muscles were actually going to burst through my skin. I knew I was close to passing out or passing away, and I prayed that God would just take me already—until I looked at Madeline. She just kept rubbing my forehead and saying, "I love you, Flex. Be strong. You'll make it."

I began cramping from head to toe, and in my terror, I put my hands over my head and began to sob. At one point, my hamstring muscles contracted so hard that my leg pulled up 90 degrees, shooting straight into the air. My fingers bent into a permanent fist, and then they began to pulsate. Madeleine grabbed them and began pulling them the other way until they stabilized.

"Just let me be!" I cried.

It wasn't that I was being brave—I was just so embarrassed because even *I* knew that I'd taken way too many diuretics. All the juice from my system had been drained, and my organs were failing. From the corner of the room, I could hear the whispers: "That's what happened to Mohammed Benaziza. You know, that bodybuilder who went into cardiac arrest and died last year."

I knew I wasn't going to make it, so I said my final prayers. Yet Robin had placed an urgent call to Jerry Brennan, a world-renowned sports-medicine specialist. The knowledge this man possesses is amazing, and he's helped many athletes get off steroids or worse. He also doesn't blame or judge—he'll just calmly tell his patient what to do to make it better right now and in the future.

Jerry arrived, took one look at me, and started forcing me to take some vitamins and minerals to counteract what the diuretics were doing. Even though my lips could barely connect with a glass for more than a minute, he made me sip as much water as I could to flush some fluids into my system. "Flex, you have *no* water in your body. You're about to go into cardiac arrest. You must drink," he calmly stated. Even when I didn't think I could breathe, he said, "Breathe later, sip now."

Thank God I listened. After a few moments, the cramping began to subside. At that point, only one thing went through my mind: *Did the show start?* "Don't think that I'm not competing," I told everyone.

I did go on that night, fully aware that I'd just escaped death again. I was told later that not even a trip to the emergency room would have stopped me from dying if I would have gone much longer without water.

I won that night, making it my second miracle of the evening. I wish I could tell you that it was a harsh lesson and I never popped a diuretic again, but that wasn't an option in bodybuilding in the '90s.

In 1996, I was in England, and this time the horrible cramping began *during* the show. It was truly mortifying, because I went down in front of all the other athletes. They saw me looking weak, and my bruised ego was worse than any physical pain. Nevertheless, my muscles began to do the hustle on their own again, and it took four competitors to carry my screaming self outside.

"What diuretic did you take, Flex?" one judge asked me point-blank.

I was straight with him. I knew I had to be honest so that he could find a solution. He gave me massive doses of zinc, magnesium, and salt, and also called for an ambulance. Usually, I'd have blown off serious medical attention, but this time I knew it was worse then ever.

The paramedics even looked worried. "It's bad, sir," one of

them said as my leg muscles began to jump off the stretcher.

The doctor in the emergency room told me that my kidneys had failed. I protested, insisting that we had to stop this nonsense because I had a competition that night. "Just get me on my feet. Get me better," I insisted. "Then someone can drive me back to the show."

"Son, your career is over and your life . . . well, it's hanging in the balance. Do you want us to get a priest?" asked the doctor. "Do you believe in last rites?"

But overnight I went from being on death's door to getting a clean bill of health. It was like I dialed 1-900-MIRACLE, and someone placed my order right away.

"Strangely, your kidneys are working perfectly fine now," the doctor said the next day. "Flex, I do want you to stay in the hospital a few days for observation," he added.

Listen? Me? Hell, no. Stupidly, I released myself against doctor's orders and went right to the airport, because if I could make the next flight to Germany then I could compete in another show. Once I was in my seat, I asked the flight attendant for some water. I wasn't trying to replenish my system or give my kidneys a little hydration—I needed the water to pop a handful of diuretics. Hey, if I was going to compete in a European bodybuilding show, then I had to look my best, right? I needed the money from the win, and even though I knew I was tempting fate, I promised myself that afterwards I'd start taking better care of my health. Life, however, had a different plan for me.

I collapsed again, and airport security had to carry me off the plane and call an ambulance. On the way to the German hospital, my muscles began to do their boogie-woogie thing all over again. I was scared out of my mind. The German doctors would come in and out of my tiny room, pull the curtain back, and talk *at* me, but I didn't have a clue what they were saying. I kept nodding my head, wondering if I was giving them permission to do something horrific to me. Was I telling them to operate? Put me on dialysis? Lop off my head? I knew I needed out of there and quickly, but this time I was stuck. I could hear the doctors placing an order to hook my kidneys up to dialysis, which they insisted through a translator was the only option for my survival. Now to an athlete, kidney dialysis is the end of your career and maybe your life.

I freaked out and called Madeleine, telling her to book the next flight to Germany. She was hysterical when she found out that life was throwing us another curve—she couldn't find her passport anywhere. It seemed like such a small detail, but it was everything to me. No passport. No Madeline. I was all alone.

Luckily, a voice interrupted my mental misery. "Mr. Wheeler, I'm Dr. Brightman. I think you've been misdiagnosed," he said. He looked like he was about 14 years old, playing a doctor in a school play—the chart in his hands looked like a prop. "I have an idea of what's really going on inside of you," he said. I don't know why, but I trusted the kid.

The boy doctor put me through 24 hours of heavy analysis and more tests than I thought they could do on a human being. I was poked and prodded, and they took blood and fluids, but my kidneys were still doing their own job so I didn't have to go on dialysis. A few more hours passed, and I continued to hold my own, which amazed the older docs. It turns out that my kidneys were working just fine, but the diuretics had caused them to temporarily shut down.

I couldn't believe it when a week later, I was finally on a flight back to Los Angeles. When I walked off the plane, Madeline ran up to me like a woman in one of those war movies who never thought she'd see her man again. "Flex, I thought I lost you," she sobbed.

I held her close, kissed her a million times, and said, "I know, I know."

Madeline never asked me why I'd taken so many pills. Many women would have passed the blame platter around, but not my wife. She knew the intense pressure I was under to compete and win, that I was a champion who couldn't let anyone down. She also knew what it took to do my job—you don't yell at a basketball player for slamming his hands on the rim of the basket, and you don't yell at a bodybuilder for taking his pills. Again, it's all part of the game.

Once I had a few days to chill, I went to my local doctor so he could make sure that I hadn't done any permanent damage. He told me that my kidneys were dry, but functioning just fine. In fact, I was told that my organs were working better than those of most so-called regular folks out there, which is the only reason I was able to make such fast recoveries during my hospital stays. So my diagnosis was simple: I'd drained my kidneys of water and overloaded on steroids, and I needed to cool it with both.

I learned my lesson and never took that many diuretics again. But as I mentioned, as time wore on, I realized that I was just physically exhausted. The player was played. I took the risks knowing that they could be fatal, and deep in my soul, I knew I'd been riding a lucky streak . . . but every gambler knows that his streak must one day end.

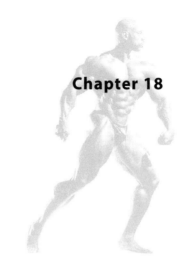

Chapter 18

By the Grace of God

One of the great blessings in my life arrived on September 23, 1998, a month after I turned 33. Darius Wheeler was a strapping seven-pound baby with a full head of hair and a smile that melted hearts. He was born with his eyes wide open and was already holding up his own head. To paraphrase my grandmother, I saw great things for this little miracle man.

Madeline and I were out of our minds with happiness, and I amazed myself with my fatherhood skills this time around. I was a maniac when it came to every detail of his checkups and shots, and I'd panic over every sniffle or case of hiccups. That's how much I loved my new baby boy.

As for my own health, I pretty much ignored it. After all, I felt perfectly fine, and I passed the short backstage physicals before the 1998 competitions with flying colors. I even peed in a cup to comply with new drug-testing rules, which everyone knew were a joke. No one ever flunked these particular tests, especially the guys who regularly won competitions.

During a short rest from training, some old friends came over and mentioned that a few nights a week they studied the Bible. They told me how this really evened out their emotions, provided the best type of comfort during the hard times, and gave them a higher purpose. I wanted to learn more, so some of the guys and I would go work out, and then for two or three hours afterwards, we'd study the Bible with a minister named Tom Brown. We'd talk about what certain passages meant to us, and the meaning of God's work started to become clear to me. It wasn't like school, where I struggled reading meaningless words; in fact, I found that once I got past the misery of dyslexia, the simple act of learning filled me with an exhilarating type of joy.

It took a while, but I eventually discovered that my general negativity started to evaporate from my system. The hole in my life caused by the abuse I'd suffered as a child was being filled with love and warmth from a power much higher than myself. It didn't take a genius to realize that I'd finally found what I'd been looking for my entire life: peace of mind.

I knew that I was finally on the right path. It was as if some powerful force put the Bible in my hand and said, "Just open it. That's all you have to do." Soon, activities that I'd once accepted as being "one of the guys" started to make me sick. I didn't visit strip clubs with my pals—I didn't want these bimbos even coming up to me. I didn't lie to anyone, and I didn't even want to swear anymore. I wanted to live a pure Christian life.

At the time, I wasn't sure if that purity could be found in the world of professional sports. Could God muscle his way in there, too?

(—)

The sports press kept insisting that I was going to win Olympia 1998. The current Mr. Olympia had retired, so there was nothing standing in my way. "Flex's name is practically on that trophy," most bodybuilding magazines insisted. And it would be—I *would* be number one.

As I trained for the competition, however, I became a prisoner of my own mind. My nagging doubts returned with a vengeance, even though I'd just won the Arnold Classic and the Ironman. I knew I had to get into the mind-set of winning, but I was almost scared to let my mind believe I could be number one. Despite my newly found faith,

I'd just lie there in the middle of the night thinking, *I don't know if I can do it. I don't know if I can be Mr. Olympia.*

These bad vibes started influencing the way I prepped for the competition. There were days when I just wouldn't train hard, or I'd break my diet. That was bad enough, but even worse was when I'd miss a workout altogether. I was like a toddler throwing a temper tantrum, screaming, "No! I just won't. And you can't make me!" I was setting myself up to fail miserably—the sad part is that I didn't realize it until it was almost too late.

A few weeks before the competition, I began to snap out of it. I got scared by what I'd been doing to myself, and then I got really pissed off. So I buckled down and began to train like a champion, but I really didn't have enough time to do the work I needed to do to win.

Olympia in 1998 was held at Madison Square Garden in New York City on a sultry fall night. I was stoked to be at the Garden—the home of so many great sporting events that it made my blood tingle. I was ready to make history at that place. Before I knew it, I was backstage at the show, staring up at the ceiling of a dressing room that had probably seen the likes of everyone from Mike Tyson to Bob Dylan. As I'd done before many shows, I tried to relax and center myself before the action swung into overdrive. The only problem was that my mind wouldn't allow itself to slip into that tranquil state. By this time, I was furious with myself because of how much I'd screwed around.

I heard other competitors complain, "Man, I'm so exhausted! I've been pushing it hard for months." I wanted to say, "Well, *I'm* not. I've goofed off this whole time, so guess what? The great Flex Wheeler has got to go out there and try as hard as he can to still be great." Instead, I said a little prayer, begging God to be my coach for the next few hours.

I had to come to terms with what I'd done to myself. *If someone else deserves the title, then so be it,* I finally told myself. But the champion in me still had a bit of fight left in him. *What makes some other guy better than I am? It's his will versus mine,* I reasoned. I came to grips with the whole situation—I'd try harder than anyone else even if my body wasn't cranked up to the max.

I ended up losing.

By three points.

I got what I deserved—a second-place trophy. I'd also have to wait another year to redeem myself, which filled me with rage. In fact, I think I spent the rest of that whole year as mad as I've ever been. Of course, everyone got a bit sick of my crappy attitude. The bottom line was that Ronnie Coleman won because he looked better. I knew I had to just face facts and suck it up. You can only point fingers so long before that one's pointed back at you. But three little points between me and Olympia gold? If I would have lost by a lot, I almost would have felt better. I was livid because if I'd given just a little bit more effort, I could have pulled it off.

Madeline didn't coddle me. "You screwed up," she said. It wasn't a brutal comment—she was just being straight up. But she was also hopeful. "You'll come back next year, baby," she assured me. "I believe in you."

Soon I began shutting out everything else but training for Olympia 1999, which would be fought at the Mandalay Bay Resort in Las Vegas that October. I could hear the announcer calling out in my head: *Flex Wheeler won Mr. Olympia! He's number one, the best body-builder in the world!* I was set on winning that trophy, and I knew the only way to do it was to push my body to the limit in a way I'd never done before. When I took a devastating second at the Pro World Championship that year and copped another second at the Grand Prix in England, I realized that I had to drive myself even harder. So I increased the dosage of steroids, lived in the gym, and only ate chicken and oatmeal. And then I performed one of the most rash training moves I'd ever done in my life—I left my wife.

Wait! I didn't divorce her. I just moved into an apartment closer to my gym for five weeks so that there would be no excuses and no distractions. My entire life was in the sweat that poured out of me during the ten hours of brutal work I punished myself with seven days a week. Madeline would come to the apartment, cook my food, and hang out for a little while at night, but then she'd go home to be with the baby. At night I'd stare at the ceiling and reflect on what I'd done wrong that day during training. As the clock inched toward midnight, I'd start to ache like crazy. Almost as a reflex, I'd turn over, expecting to have Madeline rub me down or at least comfort me with a few soothing words—but the pillow next to me was empty. My ache also came from tremendous loneliness.

It got so bad that one weekend I snuck back to my own house. "Daddy! Daddy!" Darius said as he spied me making silly faces at him in the window.

"No, honey," Madeline began, "Daddy isn't . . . Flex!"

The greeting they gave me by running into my arms was worth every single minute I'd spent away.

I figured that I deserved a little break and family time because I didn't blow off my training this time. I even did that awful cardio for three hours every single day, and sometimes I'd do a fourth hour of treadmill late at night. Let's just say that I didn't approach this at 100 percent—try 200 percent.

Robin, Rico, and I were giddy because I'd managed to put on 17 more pounds of pure muscle. "We've really got it together this time," I told Rico during one of our torturous lifting sessions.

He agreed. "Three points, my ass," he said. "They're gonna eat those three points. There is *no way* you can lose this show."

I was 246 pounds and in the best condition of my life. I went to the 1999 Mr. Olympia competition flying—and I don't just mean on the plane.

Chapter 19

Winner Takes All

I arrived in Las Vegas on a scorching Wednesday morning, carrying with me a few pounds of luggage and the eyes of a warrior. Before I went to battle, I had to weather a day of standard dog-and-pony-show stuff like interviews and a press conference: Yes, I was excited to be there. No, I didn't think anyone could beat me. No, I wasn't planning on doing any gambling while I was in Vegas. I mostly just sat there and didn't do much talking, so the press called me "Mr. Attitude." Yep, that basically took care of Thursday.

On Friday I had a light workout and some basic R&R with Madeline, her mom, and Darius. And then the next thing I knew, it was Saturday. Show time—or *showdown* time—and I was ready.

A few hours before Olympia 1999 began, I went through my standard ritual. I made sure my chicken and oatmeal were ready, and then I spent the rest of the time in my hotel room. We had a suite where one room was just for me—my sanctuary. I could walk around naked, meditate, and basically try not to fall apart emotionally. But there was no shutting off my damn mind. *I'll fight hard,* I'd assure myself; two seconds later, I'd be playing out what happened last year again and again, as if I were stuck in a torturous time warp.

"Flex, just remind yourself how hard it was to get here this year, and don't give up now," I said out loud. Great. Now I was talking to myself, which was another good reason to have a private room. "Do not under any circumstances give up," I said, like I was talking to Darius or Kennen or any other child. Then the flood of doubts would assault my brain: *Am I going to win? Is something going to go wrong? What if I pass out from nerves? What if I get those awful cramps again? Please, God, let me win.*

To silence my brain, I'd actually slap my forehead. I noticed that I had a temperature, which wasn't abnormal for me before a competition. You see, I'm the type of person who gets extremely warm if the room temperature is above 50 degrees. The cold is actually my friend in other ways, since it helps rev up the metabolism to burn fat. Yes, the Flex Wheeler Weight-Loss Plan is simple: Just move to Alaska and hang out au naturel.

"It's freezing in your sanctuary," Madeline said, refusing to come in because she joked that she and our unborn child might get frostbite. Yes, she was pregnant again, and every once in a while, she'd walk in wearing a bulky sweater over her big tummy, which was just the cutest sight in the whole wide world.

Meanwhile, I was sitting there in my underwear with no shirt on. "Madeline, come hang with me," I said.

"I'll freeze to death!" she replied.

As show time drew closer, my mood became very intense and downbeat. Madeline reminded me, "Remember how hard you've fought. Be proud of yourself because you've made it." Even better than her words was her large smile. With my hand pressed against her belly, I felt my baby moving inside of her, and I knew that winning wasn't just about me, it was for all of us.

"Let's go over the signs again," she said.

Madeline and I reviewed our secrets signs for when I was onstage and she was in the audience. But the best sign was one she couldn't give me from 100 feet away. She pressed her lips to mine and whispered, "You've already won." Her final words were direct. "I love you, Flex. I'm proud of you. Now go out there and do it!" she said with such force that I felt it in my bones. On the way out the door that day, Wonder Woman Wheeler grabbed my clothes and my gym bag and looked very sure of herself. The sight of this fired-up yet wad-dling pregnant woman made me grin.

I followed Madeline out into the hallway where a security guard was waiting to escort us to the arena. Once we hit the backstage entrance, Madeline was shown to her seat, and I was left alone.

I still had a few hours before the heat was on. "Mr. Wheeler, this is your dressing room," another guard said, holding the door open.

Here, relaxation was again the name of the game. I lay on the ground with my feet up on the wall even though there were perfectly decent couches to do my reclining. The truth is, I'm always happier at ground zero. I needed a nap really bad because I basically hadn't slept in three days. That was normal for me, because as soon as I get to any venue I'm competing in, I instantly get really sleepy. So I dozed off, knowing that I had an hour or two before I'd be called to the stage.

Boom! Boom! Boom! My nap was interrupted by loud knocks and a voice announcing, "Mr. Wheeler, you have 30 minutes until call time."

I was up like a shot, inviting one of the "oilmen" inside my dress-ing room to slick me up and make each muscle glisten. Next, a small workout seemed like a good idea, so I put myself through the paces. Light moves and stretches got my blood pumping. A few minutes later, I stopped in my tracks because I knew what would happen at any moment, and there it was—photographers and publicists had stepped inside without an invitation. They never seemed to remember to knock. I posed for a few shots, but I refused to say a word. The jour-nalists weren't shocked that I'd clammed up on them again.

At the press conference a couple of days before, my attitude had been for show. But backstage, I certainly wasn't in the mood for some gabfest, and those who knew my character didn't press their luck. The rookie reporters fired off a question or two, but one look from me shut them up. "He's such a hard-ass," one writer muttered, walking out of the room. Little did they know that I've never been one to say much before a serious competition—I'm always afraid if I open my mouth, I'll cry.

I tried to tell myself to focus and stay in the moment, but I wished that Madeline could have been there to comfort me. I wished I had another year to prepare. Another month—hell, even another day. But it was time to rock. I was pumped when I walked out of my dressing room into the great backstage area where the other bodybuilders were prowling around like caged panthers let out of their pens for the first time in a decade. We glared at each other, sizing each other up for the final kill, because this was definitely survival of the fittest.

"Five-minute warning," a stagehand called out.

Once again, it was on like Donkey Kong. The spotlights popped, music pumped through the speakers, and our names were announced. I walked onstage, and the crowd went wild. Some of my fans held banners that read: FLEX IS MR. OLYMPIA. My eyes misted but I controlled it, as I spotted Madeline, Rico, and Robin waving furiously at me.

The next thing that hit me was a wave of heat from those spotlights. Again, add 21 oversized men with very little space between them, and it was enough to mentally break me down and make me feel very claustrophobic. *It's just me out here,* I told myself. My body was screaming that it was exhausted and emotionally drained, but for once that didn't matter one lick. I was running on pure disgust. *Three points.* That's what I lost by last time. One. Two. Three. Count 'em on your fingers.

I stopped the inner dialogue at that point, afraid that I was talking to myself now, and the crowd of 50,000 could see my lips moving. *Keep it together,* I said to myself. *Don't talk. Don't exert too much energy.* But my face showed none of the above—it told the other athletes to watch themselves, because they were going down.

It was time for first call-outs, which means that we all stepped forward to do our mandatory poses.

The announcer bellowed, "As all of you know, last year there was a horrible fight for the title between Flex Wheeler and Ronnie Coleman. Will history repeat itself tonight?"

Would I kill an announcer? That was the real question. I told myself to cool it as we lined up for introductions. As my name was called amid thunderous applause, I ripped through the mandatory poses, trying not to lose too much energy on any one of them. I hit one and then calmed myself. Then another . . . and calm. Then another . . . and relax. Keeping it together through my final pose, I exited to another wave of cheers that didn't exactly make my competitors *or* me smile—they didn't grin for obvious reasons, and I didn't smile because I didn't want to tempt fate and repeat what happened in 1998.

Now it was time for the other guys to pose, which meant that I could regroup, turn my back to the crowd, ask for a drink, and let my mind go completely blank until it was time for me to go back on center stage. It wasn't easy to ignore the other guys at this show—they were the best in the world. I couldn't help but do a little mental judging of my own. I was sure that one guy looked tired and another was fighting too hard. One looked a little flabby, or was it just my imagination? Oddly enough, if I saw someone really struggling, I became his biggest cheering section. "Fight for it, man," I'd yell, surprising myself with the intensity of my voice. It's not like anyone was screaming for *me* to hang in there.

You might think that Ronnie and I were at each other's throats because he was the champion and I was there to take it all away from him. Actually, we were friends, both onstage and off. I don't care if someone is my adversary at a competition—that doesn't mean I have to hate his guts the other 364 days a year, or even on the one day we go for it. I'd finally figured out that I was there to try to give my best, and so was every other guy up there. That's just what champions do.

I went back out for the second round of posing. I looked at Madeline, who signed for me to calm down. I kept my eye on her, and she moved a few fingers. In other words, she ordered me to stay focused. I felt really confident now, and for once my brain said, *This is going really well. Man, I'm stronger than ever.*

Afterwards, there was a tiny break, and Robin and Madeline came backstage. This was the time to ask them who they thought was winning. I waited for them to say that I'd pulled into the lead, which was obvious to me.

"Flex, I'm not sure if you're winning," Madeline said.

I was shocked. I couldn't even get any words out for a moment, then I stammered, "How . . . how . . . could you possibly think that? Didn't you see what happened up there?" My jaw almost hit the floor when I saw the worried look in her eyes, a gaze that only a husband could read.

She was very composed and said, "Let's talk in private."

When we reached my dressing room, she told me what she thought I should do *and* what she thought the judges were going to do. "I think you might win, but it's very close between you and Ronnie. I'm not sure if the judges are going to allow last year's champion to lose. Everyone really likes Ronnie, and I don't think anyone has the nerve to strip his title from him."

Madeline went on to tell me that I needed to change my composure and kick things up onstage if I truly wanted to shake it up. "You need to do something big—and fast," she said.

I nodded and tried not to cry. I attempted to eat something, and took a shot at sleeping for a little while. I couldn't, so I sat there and went over every little thing I'd done onstage so far, nitpicking and driving myself crazy.

Two hours later, the routine began again. Security gave me the five-minute warning, and I was escorted back onstage for the real moment of truth. Any pro bodybuilder is aware that the judges know the scoring at this point in the show—if you're winning, they can't help but smile broadly at you when you step back onstage for the final poses. Some will even rush up and shake your hand, knowing it will be pandemonium later and they might not get a chance. But if you're not going to win, nobody wants to make eye contact with you when you return for the final showdown.

When I walked back onstage at Olympia 1999, my insides froze. *The judges looked away.*

They didn't want to silently tell me something that wasn't true, and their honesty was devastating. At that moment, I knew there were two choices—quit or hit it hard. I had a few minutes to compose myself while tech guys were fixing some of the lighting, and that's when I made my decision. *Hit it hard!* This was the first year I posed to fast hip hop. I had the beat, and now I'd really rev it up to win. So what if those judges didn't make eye contact with me? I figured that Ronnie was ahead—after all, he *was* the champion, so the odds were with him. The good news is that from my spot on the stage, I overheard some comforting whispers. A few people were saying that Ronnie was only ahead by a little, and it was very close between the two of us. At that moment, I knew that I'd be able to get this guy. I had a fighting chance since I was known to be one of the better posers in the sport, and if I went all out with my most intense routine ever and the crowd really got into it, there would be no stopping me.

I watched Ronnie go through his standard final-posing routine, which just solidified my resolve since it was the same old routine he'd done last year. It was finally my turn, so I went out there and posed like a wild man to the beat of Sean "P. Diddy" Combs. It was the most wicked routine in my life, and the crowd went berserk, to the point of giving me a standing ovation and stomping their feet in approval. There was only one thing to do at this point: I shot my fist in the air and put up a number-one sign with my index finger.

I didn't win.

Something snapped when they put that second-place medallion on my neck. I didn't know that Ronnie had, in fact, beaten me by a lot. But mentally I was beside myself, wondering how I could be going home without that first-place prize again. So when they put that medal on me, I took it off. The crowd went completely silent when I walked across the stage and pointed at myself and made the number-one sign again. A second later, I walked up to a baffled Ronnie and told him, "Hey, I don't have anything against you. Congratulations."

He got me in a hug and whispered back, "No problem, man."

The crowd booed me off the stage, and the media called me unprofessional and disrespectful. That wasn't the truth by a long shot, because I never disrespected Ronnie—we were and still are close friends. But I felt that *I* was number one in the world, and I simply wanted to express that sentiment, even though a lot of people took it in a negative way.

I've always been vocal in saying that at a contest there's a first place and a last place—nothing in-between. I want first or I want nothing. Period. I understand that a lot of people believe in their souls that it's fine to be number three in the world. I don't think that's anything close to fine. Anything less than number one is failure in my book.

That night at the 1999 Olympia amid a sea of boos, I didn't storm offstage, which is how it was reported. I walked off slowly because I was so unhappy that my feet couldn't even move right. I also knew that I was about to face a maelstrom backstage, with reporters stirring up this convoluted feud between the judges and me or Ronnie and me. My only comment that night was that the judges and I "agreed to disagree." I respected the judges, but I thought they should have voted me number one.

"But Flex, if the judges say you're number two, then don't you think you should respect that fact?" a reporter asked me.

"I *am* number one," I repeated, not meaning to diss the judges or ruin Ronnie's night. He did what he was supposed to do, and I did what I was supposed to do. I didn't want to rain on anyone's parade.

In fact, no one knew that Ronnie and I had talked about the outcome of Olympia hours before it began. "If you win, I'm not going to your party," I'd told him with a deadly serious smile.

"You know what, Flex?" he retorted. "If you win, I'm not going to your party either. But I still like you, man."

"I like you too," I said.

See, it wasn't personal. It was just two guys dealing with what was about to happen. Basically, one guy would be partying, and the other would be dying. I was the corpse in this scenario, and let me tell you, I closed that casket hard on myself. When it comes to pity parties, I can throw one that would rival any bash in Hollywood.

I was in a real funk—Ronnie had beat me, plain and simple . . . and not by three points this time. But I also knew that he hadn't completely smoked me in all of the rounds. The judges simply gave him a pass in areas where (in my humble opinion) he really didn't measure up. But he was the champion, and the rule in bodybuilding is that someone remains the champion unless someone else knocks him off. I didn't do enough to defeat Ronnie. I consoled myself with the fact that in the last 35 years of professional bodybuilding, only one champ has ever had his title ripped away. Once you get the title, it's almost yours to keep until you walk away. That's just the way of the sport.

And it's not like this is an exact science. A bodybuilding competition is like a bunch of guys going after one hot girl at a bar. The girl makes a choice, which doesn't really mean one guy is better than the other. It's just an opinion, personal and subjective. It's not about how great Ronnie was or how bad I was. I just didn't get scored in first place.

So, life was unfair, and I made sure everyone felt my pain. I flew home sad and completely depressed, a warrior licking his wounds.

My inner circle knew that the best course of action was to just leave me alone.

Only Madeline could comfort me. "Honey, you know how it is in bodybuilding," she said. "You also know that you did great. I'm so proud of you." I knew she meant it, because there were times after competitions when she wasn't so proud of me. She'd say, "You should have been in last place with that type of performance." I love that my wife is that honest, and so is Rico. Robin is more delicate, but straight up, too. At least I had people I could trust to tell me the bottom line.

Surprisingly, I came home full of piss and vinegar. Unlike other Olympias, this time I didn't take a long break to recover when it was over. I only took two weeks off, and then I hit the gym hard. I was going to start training immediately for Olympia 2000, because I needed to prove something to myself. But that was easier said than done.

Something shocking happened along the way—I took second at the Ironman in 2000. I'd won this show five years in a row, so naturally this slayed me. But I was to compete in the Arnold Classic the following week, for a first-place cash award of $100,000. The rub was that Chris Cormier, the guy who'd just beaten me in the Ironman, was also competing. The cash haul was only $10,000 for the Ironman—for the Arnold Classic, the purse was high, and I needed that money.

In February 2000, I arrived in Columbus, Ohio, for the competition, and I could sense that people were whispering about me. Everyone in the bodybuilding world knew that I was defeated and was going through this horrible, painful, soul-searching time. What they didn't know was that I was unusually determined to win back their respect. Since I only had a week to make the difference between the Ironman and the Arnold Classic, I'd really pumped up the volume. I'd done *triple* cardio sessions, which meant getting up at 3 A.M. and stepping onto my treadmill for an hour and a half each time in the sauna suit. As the sweat dripped out of every pore in my body, I'd thought about what I'd been doing wrong. I would eat, shower and fall asleep while weeping. This went on for a week. Between the tears, the sweat, the fears, and the cardio, I lost ten pounds. Consequently, I was in jaw-dropping, eye-popping, amazing shape. I was a hard man in more ways than one, and the other builders who had seen me just seven days ago were stunned. As I walked past them, I heard two words that were music to my ears: "Holy shit!"

If I show up in shape, it's tough to beat me. As soon as I walked out, the crowd started muttering, "Man, Flex is looking hot. It's over."

A few hours later, Arnold stepped up to the mike after getting an envelope from the judges. "In second place, it's Chris Cormier!"

The minute he said that name, I started crying to the point that I shook. (In fact, all the pictures of this event feature me with my face crunched up and my eyes closed.)

"The winner is *Flex Wheeler!*" Arnold screamed into the microphone. "Flex is a great champion! Let's give him a hand."

I thought I might flood the stage with my waterworks, because the tears just wouldn't stop. I knew that no one in the industry thought I could make it; plus, Madeline wasn't with me. She'd just given birth to our daughter, Nia, and the baby was sick with the flu. Robin was actually on his cell phone with her the entire time, and *he* even cried when I won. My weeping onstage really got to the crowd, because this was the first time in a long time that I'd showed any real emotion. In fact, people were freaking out and crying with me. Total strangers felt my joy and took it home with them.

Madeline was also crying at home—Robin actually climbed up onstage and let me talk to her. "I did it, honey," I said softly into the receiver.

I was really revved up for Olympia 2000, but first I had a week of exhibition shows in Budapest. These went so well that I couldn't wait to start hitting my seven-hour sessions to prep for Olympia. "If I start now, I'll be so ahead of schedule," I told Robin that spring. He nodded and smiled like we'd finally unlocked the secret to this thing. It was all about sheer willpower and guts—and who had more of that than we did?

Again, I hit the gym like a crazy person. I moved into an apartment alone to do my extra cardio, but something was very wrong. My stomach wouldn't stop hurting, and this time I knew it wasn't just nerves. On and off throughout my entire life, I've suffered through bouts of colitis (a chronic, irritable stomach problem), which is no fun—we're talking cramping, deep gut pain, and a horrible churning feeling. Right before Olympia 2000, my colitis was acting up so bad that I'd begun to lose serious weight, and not in a good way. But I flew to Vegas again, and this time I was determined to win.

"You've lost weight, Flex," the press said.

I waved them away. "I'm in the best shape of my life," I lied.

A few minutes before I got the 30-minute warning that the competition was about to begin, I felt lightheaded from my stomach problems. Right before I stepped onstage, the entire world went dark. The only thing I could do was pray: "Please, God, don't let me pass out." I was seriously thinking about walking off and withdrawing from the competition.

The judges could see that something was wrong, so they gave me a few minutes to regroup before my call-out. "Should we call a doc?" one of them asked.

I knew that this wasn't a routine problem for me, and I told myself that I didn't want to die onstage, yet I'd been through too much to just give in. Brushing past the judges, I summoned up every last ounce of strength I had and strutted out onto the stage. Immediately, I could feel my knees buckling, and I went down. Blinded by camera flashes, I felt my world going away.

"He's out," a doctor said.

"No, I'm not out. It must be these hot lights," I said.

Incredibly, I took third place that night, and I wasn't upset since I obviously wasn't in the best shape of my life. What concerned me more than my showing in the competition, however, was the knowledge that something scary was going on inside of me.

"Your electrolytes are all messed up, which is what colitis can do to you. You know, it can even kill you," the backstage doc told me.

Thinking it was just my colitis, relief flooded through me, and I went back to the hotel with my third-place trophy. That's when I did something really insane—I ordered a pizza. As I've mentioned, after my shows I always eat pizza as a treat for all my hard work, but it was a really bad idea to eat those carbs in my condition. Anyway, I thought I knew what I was doing, so after I polished off the last greasy slice of pepperoni, I put Madeline on alert. I told her that I might have a serious colitis attack at some point in the evening. But a few minutes later, I was curled up in a ball on the floor, writhing in agony. This was beyond a stomachache—my chest, arm, and leg muscles even ached from the pain.

My father, who had flown in for the show, was seriously worried about me, a fact that upset me more than my pain. "Son, don't you want to go to a hospital?" he asked.

"No!" I cried. "I can't go to a hospital—think of all the press. Dad, I just need to sit here and die."

Chapter 20

The Bottom Drops Out

Robin took charge and called an ambulance. He explained to the dispatcher who I was and that we needed to keep this extremely quiet. And when the EMTs arrived in my room, Robin told them, "We can't make a scene or Flex will be in every newspaper in the country." One thing about Vegas is that they know how to hide the bodies, so to speak. The paramedics covered me with a sheet to keep anyone from seeing me, so I looked like a dead body being wheeled through the service entrance and into an ambulance.

The EMTs diagnosed me as "extremely dehydrated," and this time it wasn't because of diuretics (I hadn't taken any). Once I reached the hospital, a kindly doctor told me, "If you'd waited a little longer, son . . . well, it wouldn't have been good." How many times in my life would I have to hear those words?

A few hours later, the hospital released me, and I went back to my hotel suite. I know you may not believe the next part, but I have to tell you the God's honest truth: I ordered another pizza. Of course, the cramping began again, but this time it was even worse than before. I tried to keep my pain from everyone else, but the next day, my colitis had kicked into overdrive. I was in so much pain that I started screaming. I even fell to my knees and begged God to stop my suffering.

Madeline, who had been sleeping in the other room of our suite, rushed to my side. I didn't want to cause her any more grief, so I just told her that I was really upset about losing Olympia again. She went back to sleep, and soon we flew home.

The minute we landed, I told her the truth: "I've been hiding it, but I feel worse than ever."

She immediately rushed me to Cedars-Sinai hospital, where I stayed for 14 days.

"You could have died from being this dehydrated from your colitis," one of the doctors told me.

"I can't die. I have to go to Rome in a few days for an exhibition," I replied.

"You're crazy," the doc retorted.

The truth is that by now I really needed the money from going to Rome because my endorsement deals were starting to dry up. After all, no one backs someone in third place. I needed to provide for my family, so I went to Rome.

One doctor put me on diuretics, of all things, to help with the trip. You see, I had a condition known as *edema,* or severe water retention, from the way I was hydrated in the hospital. "We don't want your stomach to swell up on the plane or you'll be in serious trouble. The diuretics will help with the edema," the doctor said.

That didn't sound so bad, so I went to Rome and did my appearances. But on the flight home, I looked down at my throbbing stomach and knew I was in serious trouble. The minute I landed, I called Madeline and told her to meet me at Cedars-Sinai.

A few hours later, a specialist told Madeline that I might not make it. She was devastated—she'd begged me not to go to Rome, and her worst fears were now coming true.

Even though specialists were called in and a battery of tests was performed on me, no one seemed to be able to figure out what was wrong. All they knew was that it was serious. It was then that I realized that the trophies, the mansions, and the cars meant nothing. What mattered was being around for my wife and kids.

The doctors did a lymphectomy near my hip so that they could take some tissue from the lymph nodes to really see what was cooking down there. And then the six-inch incision they made began to swell and leak.

"It's okay," I was told. "You can even go home because your vital signs are good. But come back in a couple of days and we'll check the wound again."

Unfortunately, the cut on my side began to leak so badly that I ended up grabbing a few of my daughter's Pampers to stick on the side of my hip. They got soaked so quickly with blood and pus that I had to change them every hour. I knew the wound must be infected, and it was so painful that I could barely move. However, Madeline was really sick with the flu, so I didn't want to bother her. I just stayed in bed, changing my own Pampers and trying to cope with the pain.

I was done—I was sick, my family was going broke, and my career was over. I had only one choice to save any part of my life, so I picked up the phone and dialed 911. "My name is Flex Wheeler," I said, "and I need an ambulance."

"The bodybuilder?" asked the incredulous operator.

"Yes, ma'am. Hurry," I whispered.

I have no memory of what happened next. According to Madeline, I passed out and was wheeled back into surgery for two hours. When I woke up again, I was in excruciating pain. The nurses wouldn't tell me anything, nor would they allow Madeline in the room due to her flu. They also weren't allowed to talk about "my condition." At that point, I knew it was really serious, but I'd gone through serious before in my life. I could handle it.

"We made a mistake, Flex," the doctor finally admitted to me the next day. "You have a staph infection from when we did that lymphectomy on your hip. I never realized how serious it was. We need to keep you here until it clears up."

"What's a staph infection?" I asked.

"Well, if you'd waited a little longer to come to the hospital, it could have killed you. It's the type of infection that gets into your bloodstream and essentially eats you alive," he said.

"But . . . but why . . . " The pain was almost making me pass out, and I could barely speak by now. "Why do I feel this way?" I managed.

"We had to dig deep from your buttocks to your thigh to scrape the infection out of you," the doc said. And he had even more bad news: "We still don't know what's wrong with you. We need to do a kidney biopsy, which is the only way we'll really find out what's making you feel this sick."

I refused to let these bloodsuckers hurt me even more, but Madeline quietly said, "Let them do it, Flex." For once, she wasn't Wonder Woman—she looked more scared than I'd ever seen her before.

The doctor went on to tell me that they couldn't stitch up my wound. They had to keep it open in order to dig out the infection.

"I want to see it. Now!" I demanded.

Reluctantly, the doctor lifted the gauze, and I saw a gaping hole that ran from my hip down the side of my leg and over to my butt. The bandage was a mile long. "How much goddamn tissue did you have to remove?" I cried.

"It's bad, but it *will* heal," the doctor insisted, which calmed me down for about two minutes.

It got really fun about four times a day, when a doctor and nurse would come in to remove the gauze. When the wound was exposed to air, I'd yelp in blinding pain, but what came next was far worse. They had to pack the entire area full of medicine, which was pure agony. I was exhausted, as was Madeline (who stayed with me most of the time while her family looked after the kids). At night I hallucinated that my leg was a dog, and I called out strange names. I didn't know where I was except that I wasn't at home.

The doctor then delivered some delightful news: "Flex, obviously something is wrong with your kidneys, so I need to take you off all the pain medications."

I couldn't believe it. "You're what?"

He continued, "You're hallucinating because the toxic level in your bloodstream is high and your kidneys aren't functioning right to get rid of it. Your entire body is being poisoned by the pain meds because you can't release them from your system—that's why you keep seeing such strange things in your mind."

"So what happens once you take me off the meds?" I asked, knowing that what came next was going to horrify me.

"You're going to feel *everything*," he said.

"It already kills when you pack my wound," I said.

"That will seem like nothing." His eyes misted over. "We're so sorry, but this is the only thing we can do to save your life."

The next time they came to pack my wound, Madeline had to hold my hand so tightly that I could see every vein in her face popping out. It was the first time she'd seen my wound up close, and she looked at me with tears in her eyes.

The nurse noticed her discomfort. "Mrs. Wheeler, do you want to leave?" she asked. "It's okay."

"No, I'm fine," said my brave wife, grasping my hand even tighter. "Flex, it's going to be okay. Just hold on," the woman always by my side told me. Later, I heard her yell at the doctor in the hallway: "How can anyone endure that much pain? This is inhuman!"

"His kidneys are failing and we don't know why," the doctor replied. "He can't handle any medication."

Suffice it to say, this was one of the worst times of my life, and my little family had to endure it alone. But the news finally got out, and my parents and sister wanted to come to the hospital. I told them it wasn't really that bad, but Madeline insisted that I tell them the truth.

My sister, Sharalene, said, "I'm coming. Don't tell me that you don't want me there. I don't care. I'm coming now." True to her word, she flew down from Oakland, and my father arrived a few days later.

As the week wore on, there were little bright spots that I'll never forget. For instance, Sharalene walked over to my bed one day with a big towel and a bar of soap, wanting to bathe me.

"Come on, you're my sister," I said, making a face. I just couldn't let her do it.

"Then let me do *something*," she pleaded. She ended up giving me the best manicure and pedicure in history, and it meant more to me than I can ever say.

One morning, however, the entire crew was kicked out of my room. The doctor came in and told me, "We know what's wrong with you."

Chapter 21

Am I Going to Die?

"Mr. Wheeler, we just got back the results of your kidney biopsy," the doctor said. "I'm so sorry to tell you that you have a hereditary disease called *FSGS*—or *focal segmental glomerulosclerosis.*"

I couldn't believe this was happening. "But you can treat it . . . it's not like I'm going to die, right?"

"It's a deadly disease," he quietly replied. "It's the most aggressive kidney disease known to man."

The doctor went on to tell me that FSGS is an illness that attacks the *glomerulus* (the main filtering part of the kidneys), causing protein to leak into the urine. As time passes, this protein becomes a toxin and destroys the filters in the kidneys. The damage depends on the patient—it can be progressive and slow for some or rapid for others. The scariest part of the disease is that it can progress without any symptoms, and can suddenly cause kidney failure, which means that the victim who drew this unlucky card then requires dialysis or a transplant. One day you're fine; the next you're on death's door. It mostly affects African-American males, for a reason doctors have yet to figure out.

I felt as if several bullets had just slammed through my system. "Doctors have no idea how this type of kidney disease starts, and they have no cure for it." *Boom!* "It's something that attacks the kidneys hard and just causes them to fail. Only 10 percent survive the disease. Basically, you either die of it early in life, or if you're lucky, you lose the battle later on." *Boom!*

I was crushed, out of my mind with grief, and wondering, *Why me?* And then in a moment of clarity, I had a horrifying thought. "Doc, did this happen to me because I used steroids?" I asked.

"Flex, look at me," the doc said, and I looked away. *"Kenny Wheeler, you look at me!"* he practically shouted. "Your steroid use has nothing, absolutely nothing, to do with this disease. It just comes on like hell on wheels, usually around age 25 in African-American males."

"You're sure it wasn't me?" I asked. "I didn't cause it?" My mind flashed to all those newspaper reports I'd seen about the effects of steroids and how harmful they are to the human body—how they hurt the heart and cause the internal organs to grow at a rapid speed and deteriorate as time passes. A few athletes had even lost their lives thanks to steroids—was I now losing mine because of those damn shots?

"It was *not* the steroids," the doc said. He told me about two very famous basketball players who had recently retired from the NBA very quietly because they were suffering from this disease, and they're still keeping this fact of their life a secret. He also explained that there were countless other young black males out there who tried to ignore FSGS until it was too late, and they'd never even seen a steroid. "There is a course of action," he continued, and I felt the first tiny glimmer of hope. "First, we need to control your blood pressure. Second, there's an experimental drug we've been trying. It may slow down the disease to the point where you can outlive it."

"I want it—now!" I cried.

"There are some very bad side effects to this drug," he warned, "which are more deadly in some cases than the actual disease. They include schizophrenia, tremendous swelling of the body, and extremely high blood pressure." But the doc knew what would happen to me if I didn't take the drug. By my late 30s, my kidneys would be failing; in my 40s, I'd be on a dialysis machine and praying for a kidney transplant. If I didn't get one, I'd die.

"Okay, I guess I'll try it," I said.

Madeline agreed with me. "How much of the drug does he need to take?" she asked.

"Being that the disease has entered the lethal stage, Flex will need to take more of it. And then we have to factor in the large size of your body," the doctor explained. He told us that people normally take 10 milligrams a week to keep this disease from developing into the deadly stage, but he thought I should take 80 milligrams a week. And since my leg was finally healing and the staph infection was gone, he sent me home to try a few chalky pills that were hopefully going to save my life.

Immediately, the side effects kicked in. My entire body swelled up to the point that I had a quadruple chin and a head so huge that I looked like some sort of freak-show monster. Darius would look at me and scream because my face was so inflated that my eyes were almost swollen shut. I looked like Eddie Murphy as Sherman Klump in *The Nutty Professor* movie, only no one was laughing. I didn't even recognize my own reflection in the mirror.

During this time, we had Nia's first birthday party. I couldn't go downstairs and frighten the other children, so a family friend and makeup artist came over and painted my face into the image of a lion. The kids loved it, but I was in agony as I wondered if I'd see my daughter's second birthday.

My entire body also broke out with severe acne. I started having intense panic attacks, and suicidal thoughts poured through my head again. I'd stand on the top floor of our house, thinking about jumping out a window. "Someone's trying to kill me!" I'd yell to Madeline.

I heard voices that ranged from demons to my grandmother begging me to join her. I finally asked Madeline to explain what "schizo" meant. "In your head, you're scared of yourself," she explained.

I couldn't take it anymore, so I went back to the hospital, where I was told that the drugs were killing me, so they needed to take me off of them at once.

The doctor looked so upset. "Flex, at your body weight, you should be on 120 milligrams a week of this drug, and obviously your body can't even handle 80."

"Now what?" I asked. I'm of the generation where there's always another option. But the game was over—my body was played out.

"We gave it our best shot. I told you that the drug isn't 100 percent," said my doc. He'd run out of ideas, and I'd run out of options.

"Now what?" I repeated. "I'm not the type of man who just sits it out and waits." After all, this was the Olympia of life, and I'd never once shied away from a challenge.

The doc appreciated my fighting spirit, and it turns out that he did have a few tricks left up that white sleeve of his. "Now we control your blood pressure, which will help," he said. He put me on four blood-pressure meds that I'd have to take every single day. Also, once a week I was to come in for tests that would check the toxic level of my kidneys.

I kept expecting a miracle, and prayed hard for one, but my kidneys got worse and worse as each week passed, and the toxic levels increased. Robin and I put together a press release that went out to the sports media and was posted on my Website. At the time, I chose not to go public with the disease because I didn't know enough about it to talk about it in a way that could help others. I also knew that I was a big inspiration to those brothers battling their way off the streets, and the last thing they needed was to watch another dream die. So I kept my disease a secret, knowing that if I found some way to avoid just lying in a corner and dying, then maybe I'd talk about it. Back then, my official response was simple: "Champion Flex Wheeler has decided to retire from bodybuilding to tackle other pursuits! Check this Website often for his exciting new endeavors!"

My "endeavor" was survival. I decided to finally let my brother Darnell in on what was going on. This wasn't easy. Remember when I told you that I thought Darnell was getting into trouble? Well, I was right. My brother was and is currently incarcerated for reasons both of us have decided to keep private. It's his story to tell someday—not mine. But I thought that he might be a match for a kidney transplant since we have the same blood type.

Darnell was only too happy to go in for the tests, and the state of California allowed this to happen. "Whatever you need, Kenny," he cried. "I love you and would give you anything." All those years ago when we were sharing that garage bedroom and he was picking on me, who would have thought that Darnell would one day turn out to be my angel?

It killed him that he wasn't a match. "Let's try it anyway. Just take my kidney, and maybe it will work," he said.

I began to cry, because it was so touching. I had to explain to him that the wrong kidney would certainly kill me, and the operation could kill him.

"If you ever want to try it, I'm there for you," he said.

Meanwhile, every single week I went to see the doc so he could keep checking my kidneys. One week they'd be in trouble, and the next, strangely better. Then they would improve two weeks in a row, and then for a month. The doctor was in disbelief. "I think we'll let you go a month and then monitor you again," he said.

Four weeks later, he was at a loss for words. He finally said, "You seem to be completely healthy, Flex. Your levels are back to normal. Even I can't believe this—I expected you to be on dialysis by now. What are you doing?"

I think he thought I was going to explain some voodoo spell or name the mineral water I was sipping or the herbal drugs I was downing. "What I'm doing is praying," I said. "That's all I'm doing." That was the truth. Many times a day, I asked God to just let me live to see my kids grow up.

My doc just shook his head.

"I guess I *am* a miracle, and this is Jesus' will," I said.

To which the doc replied, "Well, I'm Jewish."

I laughed and said, "So was Jesus."

My doc smiled and said, "If you keep getting better, I'm going to have to agree with you about the miracle part!"

Chapter 22

The 10th Percentile

By the grace of God, I'm one of the lucky ones who has survived FSGS. As I mentioned, only about 10 percent of people who contract this disease do. However, there's no cure for it, so it continually lurks like some sort of devil in the night. It takes a strong man to fight the devil, but I've got help from my amazing doctor, who tells me just about every week, "You continue to amaze me."

It was really hard to live with this secret. I was afraid that as an athlete, I couldn't show any weakness. And as I write this book, I have new fears. You see, I could produce 100 signed forms from doctors that show otherwise, but I know that regular folk are still going to think that I got this horrible disease because I took steroids for two decades.

"I'll tell, show, or scream it to anyone who listens that you did *not* get FSGS from steroids!" my doc always tells me.

I love him for this, but I still want to tell my fans that I wish I'd never touched a steroid. And these days, I beg young athletes to stay away from them because of various health problems that don't include FSGS.

Steroids are dangerous—period. They're lethal. Listen to me for just one minute: It only makes sense that if your muscles are growing at a rapid speed, so is everything else inside of your body . . . including your vital organs. Eventually those organs will start to shut down because they weren't meant to grow that large, and then the effects are irreversible. *You will die.* In my case, my organs are miraculously normal (except for my kidneys, thanks to the FSGS). Still, I'm a warning to everyone out there that you should compete solely with your God-given attributes—after all, the only true win in this life is good health.

As for FSGS, check out the Websites (if you type in "FSGS" in a search engine on the Internet, about a dozen sites will come up). You'll find out that this disease is very prominent in black men, which is probably why there's been little research done; it can bring on AIDS-like symptoms; and certain foods can aggravate the condition—for example, most fruit is very hard on the kidneys, so I avoid it (but I do drink cranberry juice). The information is still sparse, and that's why I've decided to speak out.

From my career in bodybuilding, I have records of my kidney function over the years. From the time I was 20, I've been losing protein, which is an early symptom of FSGS. When I was so sick with that staph infection in 2000, I lost 16 grams of protein a day, which is horribly dangerous.

I honestly thought I was dying, so I was depressed 24 hours a day. Then it occurred to me that maybe we need to *earn* this life we're given. I thought that maybe I should give something up—you know, bargain with a Greater Power—to stay alive.

Well, I didn't have a lot to give. As you all know, I don't use recreational drugs, I don't party, and I don't drink. So what could I give? I realized that I could give my *life* over to God. So I changed a few things in my day-to-day existence, such as switching to a low-sugar, low-sodium, and low-fat diet. But the main thing I did was to learn to savor each and every day of my life. Knowing that something is lurking in my body makes me take all the minutes of my life more seriously. On most mornings, I say, "Thank you, God, for turning me around so that my kids have a great father, and my wife can respect the man she married."

The bottom line is that FSGS could come back hard, or I could live to be 110. I think we all learned after September 11, 2001, that we could be gone tomorrow or the world could continue to spin for another million years. Hey, we're all going to die, let's face it—but I decided that I was going to live as a man of honor while I'm here. I'm filled with the spirit of a loving God who tells me that dying isn't the worst thing in the world, and if I live right, I'll get to be with Him someday.

So far, I've survived the most aggressive kidney disease known to man, which is a miracle. I honestly believe that what saved my life was giving it to God. I needed to learn to lean on Him. I've learned to find happiness in the worst of situations. I became thankful for my parking tickets, the spilled milk on the floor, and Nia and Darius whacking each other over the head with their toys. I learned to be grateful for the fights with Madeline, the electric bills we struggled to pay, and the pipes that burst in the basement to the tune of $4,000 in repairs.

Yeah, money was a problem again. When I got off the juice and out of the business, my endorsement company dropped me, so we were broke. We had to sell our nice house—can you imagine moving while your husband is battling a fatal disease?—but Madeline was great about the entire thing. "I'll get a job and support us. Don't worry about anything," she said. "Stay relaxed."

So I did, even as we had to turn in the Mercedes and the BMW because we couldn't afford the payments. For a long time, I had no steady financial means, and I know I'm not the first athlete to tell that story. One day your mug is on a box of Wheaties; the next you're just some guy trying to pay the phone bill.

The sad truth is that poor kids like myself tend to lose their minds when they get a little money. And then, when that little bit of money turns into a *lot* of dough, they're in full-on lobotomy mode. I had no clue when it came to money management, and I laughed at anyone who tried to get me to save it. I also had something else that's lethal when it comes to dealing with cash: low self-esteem.

I tried to purchase pride, and I wasted money *and* part of my life in the process. God showed me that I didn't need to brag that my driveway was an eighth of a mile long or that my house had all the latest security fences and surveillance. Having a nice day with my family in the park or seeing a new picture that Nia had drawn for me were things to brag on. So what if I didn't have a huge patio with a built-in fireplace/barbecue pit and a pool with a Jacuzzi and a waterfall? I had a Weber grill and a small plastic pool, which the kids loved putting big Daddy in and watching the water run all over the grass.

And once again, the kindness of strangers left me awestruck. Our church asked how they could help, so I told them that I couldn't afford my medical insurance. They helped pay for it—no questions asked.

At the same time, some of the church's members suggested that I might find some comfort in their Bible study classes. I think a few folks in the congregation were surprised to see an athlete in their midst at the International Church of Christ, where I've remained a devout and practicing Christian. Madeline has become just as spiritual as I have. We actually devote several nights a week to this part of our lives, and even attend weekly couples classes at the church. In a way, we're training another part of our beings—our spirits. And you know how I am about training. I'm relentless.

And speaking of training, I decided to come out of retirement to train for Olympia 2002—without steroids.

Years ago, when I first started bodybuilding, I opened my mouth and said something that has been quoted many times in gyms across America and on the Internet. I don't exactly remember which journalist had asked me to describe the important things in my life, but I gave him one of my patented hard stares and said, "I eat. I sleep. I train. Period."

As the competition neared, I was struck by how my short list of life's true goals had changed. If that person had asked me that same question as I headed to Olympia 2002, I would have said, "I pray. I love. I hope for the future. Period."

I was really looking forward to participating in the first natural (without steroids) competition of my bodybuilding career. I may have looked and felt better than ever, but I was about to face the toughest battle of my professional life.

✣ ✣ ✣

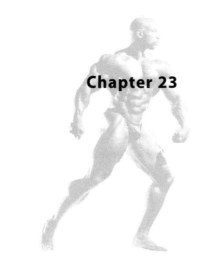

Chapter 23

Olympia 2002

I arrived in Las Vegas for my comeback in October 2002. I was 37 years old and full of hope, and the smile on my face had a little bit to do with the irony of the situation. I mean, when you're not a sinner anymore, do they allow you into Sin City?

Obviously, the answer is yes, because I was soon sitting in a suite at the Mandalay Bay Hotel with Madeline, Nia, and Darius. We'd brought along enough high-protein food to fill the refrigerator, a George Foreman grill, and a copy of the new *Scooby-Doo* movie for the kids, who didn't understand that this competition was a big deal for Daddy. Basically, Nia and Darius wanted to watch videos and swim in the pool. Score one for the kids—they knew how to live right.

Madeline had made the living-room area extra cozy by lighting a few pumpkin-scented candles. Two-year-old Nia was dancing around the room, grabbing my hand, and forcing me to join her. So I scooped her up and did a little impromptu boogie, which cracked Madeline up. Gone were the days of angst, where I paced my room like a caged panther before the competition. This was a family effort, and I had my team at my side—and on my toes. As Nia stood on top of my feet, we did a little waltz.

Joining us were six members of my church group, who had saved up and made the trip together. Their kindness just blew me away. All of us held hands in a prayer meeting, and I listened to a story about how God never allows his children to go into battle with less than they need to survive and prevail. I love that story. After the last "Amen," one of my church friends said, "We're here to support you. All you've gotta do is ask."

Again, tears came to my eyes, but they were soon replaced by amazement. Madeline's parents arrived, and her mom made a little announcement: "I just won $300 on the slots downstairs—maybe this is a good sign!"

And then Rico burst through the doors of my suite. "What's up, Dawg?" he asked, as we hugged.

Exhausted from all the training and excitement, I went to take a little nap and woke up to find that my sister, Sharalene, was sitting on my bedside holding my hand. "I'm so proud of you, Kenny," she said. I squeezed her hand back.

As we talked and reminisced a bit about old times, we heard a crash come from the other room. My 13-year-old son, Kennen, had arrived, and he was obviously roughhousing with 4-year-old Darius. When I walked into the other room, I saw that *Robin* was the one responsible for the roughhousing. I couldn't help but laugh.

"Hi, Daddy!" Darius yelled.

"Can we have pizza?" Kennen chimed in.

"The pizza has to wait until the show's over," I said, enjoying the scene before me—and how much my life had changed in two years.

The first night of Olympia is always a meet-and-greet with the fans, and I worried if mine would even remember me. I sat with the other bodybuilders at various little booths inside the convention center, and I quickly realized that I had nothing to worry about at all. The doors opened at 7 P.M., and before I knew it, more than 3,000 people had lined up to shake my hand and get my autograph.

"Flex, I have a picture of you next to my bed," one guy in his 20s told me, as tears filled his eyes. "Every day when I wake up, you're the first thing I see. You're my motivator."

"I got you these chocolate-covered macadamia nuts," said a pot-bellied man in his 40s who immediately realized that I wouldn't be having candy tonight.

"Thanks, man. Definitely for after the show," I said, laughing as Nia jumped on my lap and Darius ran through the fan line screaming, "I'm Batman!"

"Flex, you look perfect!" a prim-looking lady in her 30s exclaimed.

"You look so lean and mean," a guy in a wheelchair noted. "What are you doing?"

"I'm lean, mean, and *clean,*" I told him with a grin.

The next day contained even more fan-de-monium, and I chose that time to unveil my new philosophy to the fans. I didn't say it, I wore it. I arrived at the morning autograph session in a white T-shirt that gave my views on steroids in just a few words: FLEX WHEELER. THE NATURAL BODY. BUILT ON CONVICTION.

As I looked across the gargantuan convention hall, I saw young bodybuilders who clearly didn't get it, because they were spewing the same cocky shit that I spat out years ago. A large guy with no neck sported a T-shirt of his own, which read: IT'S NOT THAT BODYBUILD-ING IS THE GREATEST. IT'S JUST THAT BEING WEAK AND PUNY SUCKS.

Shaking my head, all I could think was, *Man, there are a lot of things in life that suck far worse than being puny,* but I didn't say any-thing. Hell, back in the day, *I* wouldn't have listened to me. There's so much in life that you have to figure out for yourself, and I knew this dude had a lot of growing up to do.

Before I knew it, the morning of the competition arrived. I woke up and said my prayers, knowing that what happened next was in God's hands. I put on my contest clothes—black posing trunks cov-ered by a new black Michael Jordan sweat suit—and thought back to my first competition as a kid when I went out there in my under-wear. I had to smile.

Madeline was up early, and let me just tell you that she was the bomb in beautiful white pants and a flowered top. She was going to get the kids ready, so the next time I saw her would be in the audience, where she'd be giving me those secret signals we had. She held me close and reminded me of something. "I don't love you because you're Flex Wheeler the bodybuilder," she said. "I love you because of the man you've become, which has everything to do with why we're here."

I kissed her good-bye, knowing that the man I face in the mirror each morning wouldn't have existed without her.

That man also had to go to work.

One thing about Mandalay Bay is that the hallways are extremely long, so, like gladiators going off to battle, all 25 of us competing at Olympia walked the gauntlet together. I saw competitors like Kevin Levrone, Chris Cormier, and, of course, Ronnie Coleman, who was still champion. Ronnie and I actually ended up in the same elevator on the way down to the convention center and each of us made a fist . . . but it wasn't to swing a punch at each other. In almost a loving way, both of us touched knuckles and said, "Good luck, brother."

"Welcome to the 38th annual Mr. Olympia," Joe Weider announced to the screaming crowd. And once again, it was on like Donkey Kong.

All of the athletes came out to thunderous applause and stood in a long line. Three of us would be called out to step forward onto a podium and do a few poses. Anyone who knows the sport knows damn well that the first three guys called out by the judges are basically the winners. Bodybuilding is sort of anticlimactic in that way.

Of course, Ronnie was called out because he was champ. I waited to be second.

Chris Cormier was called.

I prayed I'd be third.

Kevin Levrone was asked to step forward, and my heart sank. Yes, I'd come a long way, but the competitor in me still liked to win a fight. There was nothing I could do but sadly watch while the three of them went through their standard poses. I took a deep breath and prepared to be called in the next grouping, which would mean that I had a lock on fourth, fifth, or sixth place.

To my own amazement and the shock of the crowd, I wasn't called out in the next group. More sorrow washed over me, although my face had to remain a blank slate. Finally, the judges had me step forward in the third group of men vying for seventh, eighth, and ninth places. In my mind, I had only one simple thought: *This is awful!* Yet, knowing I had a job to do, I went through the standard first-round poses, reminding myself with each movement that this was the first time I was competing naturally. I was 25 to 75 pounds lighter than some of the other guys—but they weren't Flex Wheeler.

In the crowd, I heard one voice come through loud and clear: "That's my dad! That's my dad!" Kennen screamed.

I looked out in the audience and saw that my son wasn't sitting in his seat—he was jumping up and down on it. I also saw Madeline smiling widely, nodding that my poses were perfect.

I stepped back in line—and then something strange happened. The judges called me out to pose with the athletes in the next round, with the guys who'd come in tenth, eleventh, and twelfth. Again, I went through the mandatory poses, and I was beyond tired now. We stepped back, and the judges wanted to see the guys in the next class—and I was called out again. Then they wanted to see the guys in the fourth, fifth, and sixth spots, and I was asked to return to the podium, which was unprecedented. It was apparent that the judges didn't know what to do with a leaner and cleaner Flex.

By the time the first round was over, I was lightheaded. We took a short break, but I couldn't nap because I had to do a photo shoot. Then it was time for the evening finals. I walked the long hall-ways of Mandalay Bay again, knowing that everyone must have thought I was beyond depressed since I hadn't been called out in first, second, or third place. Sure, I was disappointed, but I'd made my peace with God. I knew in my own heart that it was a miracle I could even compete at all.

Backstage, that miracle wasn't obvious to everyone else. "Condolences to you, Flex," said one very famous competitor who shall go nameless.

"Say what?" I replied.

"Doing it natural is your death sentence in this sport," he said, and it was obvious that he felt sorry for me.

If he only knew what the word *condolences* could have meant to my family. And I found that *I* felt sorry for *him*. "God bless you in your future," I said, knowing that one day soon he'd be wishing he'd never given himself that first shot.

Another guy came up and said, "I'm really impressed that you dared to do it natural. I don't think I'd have the guts."

"I pray that someday you do," I responded. Then I added with a smile, "Actually, *your guts* are going to pray that you have the guts."

"I'm not feeling so well these days. I'm scared that after all these years of steroids . . . " he trailed off.

"I know, I know," I said, patting him on the back.

I went back onstage. At this point, the only thing I could do to turn it all around was my three-minute, individual posing program, which I'd crafted as a love letter to my fans.

I walked out to Whitney Houston's version of "I Will Always Love You," and after a few poses, I ripped off my black posing trunks to reveal all-American red-white-and-blue shorts underneath.

The crowd went ape-shit, and I could see some people standing to salute. Then I upped the energy with the opening strains of the hit Emenim song "Without Me," but I tweaked the words. So, instead of the rapper asking, "Guess who's back?" I'd dubbed in a joyous, "Flex is back!"

I gave the crowd every ounce of energy I had, and I pushed my body to the limit by ending my program with the splits, which got a roar of approval.

In the end, I came in seventh and Ronnie was still champ.

Was I a wreck? Did I want to throw myself off a building? Hell, no. My emotions were all over the place, but it wasn't like before, when I had to prove I was number one. I'd be lying if I said that I wasn't thrown by the final decision because I hadn't expected those early multiple call-outs. Then again, I didn't deliver the big he-man look they obviously wanted at Olympia 2002.

"Are you disappointed?" a journalist asked me backstage.

"I'd be disappointed in *myself* if I didn't accept that this is the way it was supposed to happen. God has been really good to me," I said.

This guy looked at me like I was nuts, but if he only knew. . . .

Now that it was all over, all I could think about was getting back to my hotel suite because it was Madeline's 30th birthday. Earlier I'd ordered pizzas (of course), and Robin had decorated the room with tons of streamers and signs.

When I came through the door, Kennen ran at me like a little missile. "Don't retire, Daddy! You can do it! You can win again!" he said, hugging me with all his might.

"Don't worry, buddy. I'm just getting started," I told him.

During the competition, there was a televised Internet poll, and it does my heart good to know that the fans voted me number three. However, the judges just didn't see it. In the most important way, I came clean, but I couldn't possibly have won Olympia 2002. I gave up the pounds that only steroids can put on your hide. (What's funny is if you look at the Olympia winners from the 1970s, few would stand a chance of winning now because they wouldn't be considered big enough.) In the madness to find the biggest of the big guys, no one wanted to hear the story of my dropping steroids for my health. The judges wanted a superman, and screw the fact that such a man might drop dead hours after the trophy had been placed in his needle-holding hands.

At Olympia, a few journalists from muscle magazines approached me for private conversations. "Flex, you've got to go to the hospital, get yourself tested to prove you're not on steroids, and then sue the organization," one of them insisted. "It could be a precedent-setting case, because I think you were one of the *only* guys up there who wasn't using." He added, "The reason why this sport won't ever be in the Olympics is because the people in charge of it piss all over their own rules. Supposedly, competitors can't use steroids, yet the judges just ignore the fact that the guys are using."

I listened carefully and even agreed with some of what he'd said. But when it comes to lawsuits, well, my mind just isn't there. I know that life is too short to spend in courtrooms.

It does kill me when I think about how easy it is to beat all the so-called health tests they have before a bodybuilding competition. I see other young guys who are clearly using steroids, diuretics, and worse, and they're hurting their bodies just to win an award. I hope

189

that a few of those guys read this book and have a second thought before swallowing a pill or giving themselves a shot.

I could have been the old, huge Flex with 75 more pounds on me if I was still using, but then I would have been parking my trophy on a hospital nightstand—or on top of a dialysis machine. Believe me, when your body is hooked up to all those wires and tubes and you're fighting for the next breath, you'll do anything to take it all back. Drawing a breath becomes much more important than drawing that fluid into the needle.

My belief is that Christ is the ultimate judge, not the panel of guys who give you points for poses. I don't hold myself up to their standards anymore—I hold myself up to Jesus' scrutiny. He's one judge you can't kid, and you can't cheat him either.

I do feel like I've done my part in getting the ball rolling when it comes to cleaning up this sport. To anyone who would listen at Olympia 2002, I talked about how good it felt to be a "natural" athlete. In the end, the sport must support the athletes, just like the athletes support the sport. If I changed just a few minds that weekend about steroids, or convinced one young athlete to stay clean, then I did my job. I can't stop bodybuilding from spiraling out of control, but I *can* get my message across, one athlete at a time. Battles like this are won in small steps—one day maybe I'll wake up and know that somehow I've also won the war.

As for Kennen's concern, no way am I retiring. I've only trained natural for two years, and my doctor has given me the okay to keep going because my kidneys are (thankfully) cooperating. My mind is clear, and I want to see where this natural training takes me. It never ceases to amaze me when other athletes come up to me in the gym locker room with "a great idea," telling me that I'm in such good shape now that if I started using again, I'd knock 'em dead.

I'll never go back. In fact, I have a new motto: *I compare myself only to myself.* I assume responsibility. I am no more than my Lord allows.

Living with that new credo means that these days I find myself smiling too much . . . nah, there's no such thing as smiling too much.

☦ ☦ ☦

EPILOGUE

We spend our entire lives sizing things up. As little kids, we long to be big. And when we grow up, we need *other* things to make us feel big—big bucks and big possessions. We don't admit it, but in our race to be the largest, we actually feel very small. I certainly understand that feeling. But if we're lucky, such feelings eventually lead us to the revelations of true greatness.

It's rather obvious that I wouldn't be alive without Madeline, because she owns my heart and watches my back. And my children are my treasures. My gorgeous little babies, Nia and Darius, run into my room each morning to pull the covers off of me, and I smother them with kisses. (And I'm a much more patient father this time around.)

My beautiful Brandy is 22 now, and our relationship is great. She might be moving close to me soon (yes, I'm pushing her a bit—hey, I'm her dad), and we've mended all past wounds because it doesn't pay to let those things fester. We had a lot of building to do, and it wasn't easy, but our relationship is one of the most worthwhile achievements of my life. I can't tell you the joy I felt in my heart when Brandy called me out of the blue one day to talk about some of the problems in her life. Just to know that she trusts me means everything and more.

Kennen is a smart, handsome, warm-hearted 13-year-old who doesn't mind when his father holds his hand (as long as none of his buddies are around). We're super close, and he loves to watch me train—but I'd never push him in any athletic direction. The only thing I want him to be is happy.

My mother and her wig collection still live in Fresno, where she takes care of the elderly. We talk as much as possible. Daddy (still dubbed as "so fine" by women) also lives in Fresno and works at the local rec center. A year ago, I finally told him how Crystal molested me when I was a boy. For a long time my father was speechless, and then I heard sobbing over the phone line. He told me that he hadn't had a clue and that he wished that he'd stayed at home more, but he never figured that the biggest danger to me lurked in his own home. I told him that I didn't blame him, but I wanted to share this with him before he read about it in this book.

My fantastic sister, Sharalene, runs a day-care center for autistic kids in Oakland, and she's a superstar in my eyes, because her heart is miles long and so is her mind. She's the keeper of the Wheeler family's past, and anytime I need precise details of our history, I call her up for a lesson. I'm not as close with my brother Michael, who left Fresno at 15 to go off and find his own life. Today he's an airplane mechanic who lives in Oregon. Robert works in Los Angeles as a trainer at a gym. As I said before, Darnell is incarcerated, but I long for the day that I walk out of the gym and see him leaning against my car again with a big smile on his face.

Grandmommy's still my angel.

I honestly believe that all good things are possible through sacrifice and faith. When I came out of retirement, my endorsement deals rolled back in, and my family is doing fine financially. Another prayer answered. We even have some left over to give back to our church.

Kids ask for my advice, and I go to schools and churches to lecture kids on the danger of steroids and other performance-enhancing drugs. Now I love to answer questions, and I never shrug fans off. People also come up to me and say that they remember me from various competitions, but the truth is I'm not interested in looking back when it comes to my body of work. This time I'm building the future.

Here's what I'm talking about: Darius walked up to a neighbor the other day and pointed at me mowing the lawn. "That's my Daddy," he said. "Someday, I'm gonna be like my Daddy. He's the bestest Daddy in the whole wide world 'cause he loves me."

His words are my trophy, and I keep it on a different mantel—the one inside my heart. Yet in my head, I often think back to the past.

I was 14 when I first tried to kill myself. It was a really long time ago, but it seems like yesterday—especially when I close my eyes late at night and the dream begins. And then I see my grandmother, the smallest "big woman" on the planet pulling me back from the abyss.

The first time I tried to kill myself, I drove my wobbly red moped up Highway 41 in Fresno. The other day, I took out my red Harley and drove it down the 101 Freeway in Los Angeles. Funny, but a huge Mack truck was on my tail the entire time, and I realized there was only one thing to do: I darted out of his way.

I didn't want to slide off into oblivion anymore. Instead, I slid to the off-ramp and pointed my bike in the direction of home. Toward life. *My* life.

My name is Kenny "Flex" Wheeler, and my story is just beginning.

FLEX'S LIFE-TRAINING TIPS

People are always asking me for workout pointers, and so here are some of my favorites. But let me just provide one disclaimer: The following tips will have nothing to do with developing bigger muscles—they will have to do with how to work things out in your life, your mind, and your heart. Believe me, you *will* sweat . . . just maybe not on the outside.

1. (From my grandmother, Ethel Pearl Wheeler): "I've seen horrible things in my life, but I refuse to hate anyone. I don't believe in prejudice or the differences between the races. I believe in God and love."

2. After September 11, 2001, many of us in the United States have found it very easy to hate when it comes to anyone beyond our country's borders. Sure, there are evil people in this world, but the good, God-fearing ones outnumber them—and many of these people live in conditions that we can only imagine. Instead of fearing outsiders, the best thing to do is embrace them, because we're all looking for love, acceptance, and hope.

3. Find the one thing that you're good at in this life, and then push yourself out onto the stage that is the world. You might be scared, but that's the idea. Fear is a great motivator.

4. You've got to be in it to win it. You won't get anything from just sitting home and fantasizing—you have to put your dream into action. Even though I told myself I wasn't worthy of being a champion bodybuilder, I forced myself to pursue my dream.

5. Why is it that we don't appreciate the smallest miracles of life—like walking, breathing, and smiling—until they're almost taken away? If we spent just one minute a day being glad to be alive, it would make all the difference.

6. Very few of us accomplish anything alone in this life. In order to fly, you need an extremely good crew, which is something I've been blessed with in my life. I've soared with people who were happy to help me with the lift-offs and the landings without ever taking any credit. Take a minute to give *your* support crew their props and say thank you.

7. At the worst times, you need to reach out for help, for when you're at your weakest is when the strength of others will be your only salvation. And it's then that God will send His angels to be by your side. I know that for a fact each time I look at my wife.

8. Why is it that a family member has to go down before we all rally together? Why can't we stick to each other like glue in the good times? Vow to get together with your family and form memories that aren't painful to recall years later. You'll never be sorry.

9. When it comes to your life, first place is God, next comes your family, and then you—in that order. It doesn't take a trophy or a big house to make you a winner—you're a world-class champion if you have the big three covered.

10. When in doubt, you can simply pray it out. Sometimes it's the only option . . . and it's the best one of all.

ABOUT THE AUTHORS

Kenny "Flex" Wheeler is one of the top bodybuilding champions in the history of the sport. His amazing form has been seen frequently on ESPN, in the pages of *Sports Illustrated,* and several bodybuilding magazines. He's in the *Guinness Book of World Records* for his multiple wins of the Arnold Classic, sponsored by Arnold Schwarzenegger, who has dubbed Flex "one of the best bodybuilders of all time." Flex is also a personal trainer to some of Hollywood's elite. In his spare time, Flex is very devoted to his local church—he's made it his mission to warn kids and fellow athletes about the dangers of using steroids or other performance-enhancing drugs. Visit Flex's Website: **teamflex.com.**

Cindy Pearlman is a nationally syndicated writer for the *New York Times Syndicate* and the *Chicago Sun-Times.* Her work has appeared in *Entertainment Weekly, Premiere, People, Ladies' Home Journal, McCall's, Seventeen, Movieline,* and *Cinescape.* Over the past 15 years, she has interviewed Hollywood's biggest stars, who appear in her column "The Big Picture." Cindy is also the co-author of *Simple Things* (with Jim Brickman) and *It's Not about the Horse* (with Wyatt Webb).

We hope you enjoyed this Hay House book.
If you would like to receive a free catalog featuring
additional Hay House books and products,
or if you would like information about the
Hay Foundation, please contact:

Hay House, Inc.
P.O. Box 5100
Carlsbad, CA 92018-5100

(760) 431-7695 or (800) 654-5126
(760) 431-6948 (fax) or (800) 650-5115 (fax)
www.hayhouse.com

Published and distributed in Australia by: Hay House Australia
Pty Ltd, 18/36 Ralph St., Alexandria NSW 2015
Phone: 612-9669-4299 • *Fax:* 612-9669-4144
E-mail: info@hayhouse.com.au

Published and Distributed in the United Kingdom by:
Hay House UK, Ltd. • Unit 202, Canalot Studios
222 Kensal Rd., London W10 5BN • *Phone:* 020-8962-1230
Fax: 020-8962-1239

Distributed in Canada by: Raincoast • 9050 Shaughnessy St.,
Vancouver, B.C. V6P 6E5
Phone: (604) 323-7100 • *Fax:* (604) 323-2600